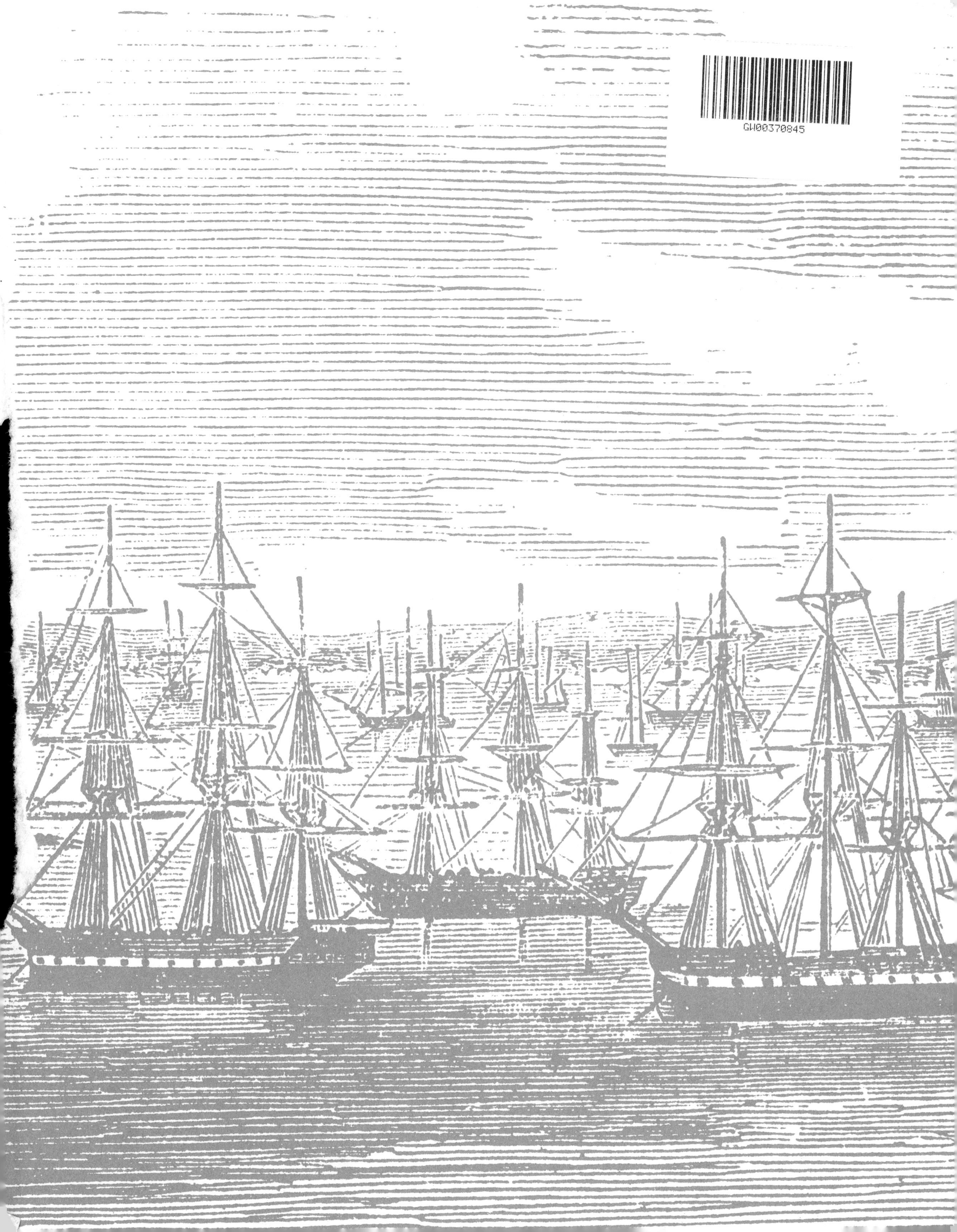

AUSTRALIA

FLINT RIVER

FLINT RIVER PRESS LTD.
26 Litchfield Street
London WC2H 9NJ

AUST

Text and captions by

KENNETH McKENNEY

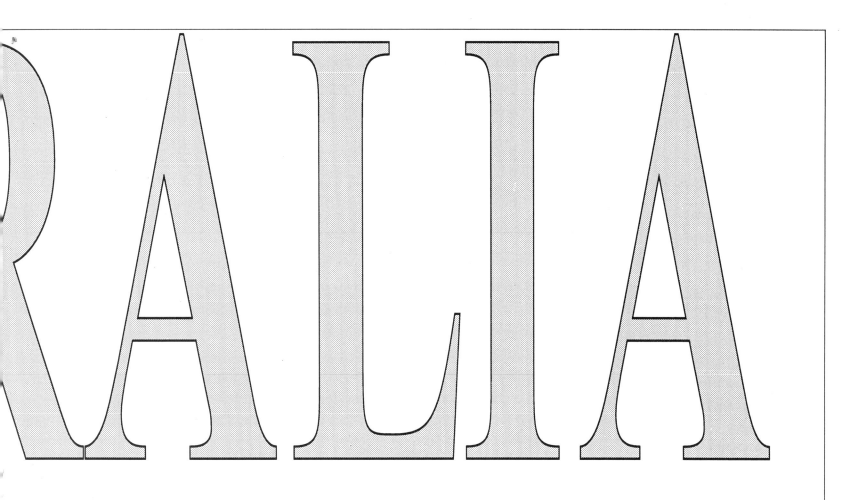

RALIA

Photographs by

GUIDO ALBERTO ROSSI

A Motovun Group Book

© Flint River Press Ltd 1993

First published in the U.K. by

FLINT RIVER PRESS Ltd
28 Denmark Street, London WC2H 8NJ

ISBN: 1 871489 14 8

Originated and developed by
Bato Tomasevic

Design
Gane Aleksic

Editor
Madge Phillips

Additional photographs
Nos. 141, 197, 198 by
Robert Harding Picture Library

Typesetting by Avalon
Printed and bound in Slovenia by
Tiskarna Ljudska Pravica, Ljubljana

CONTENTS

AUSTRALIA

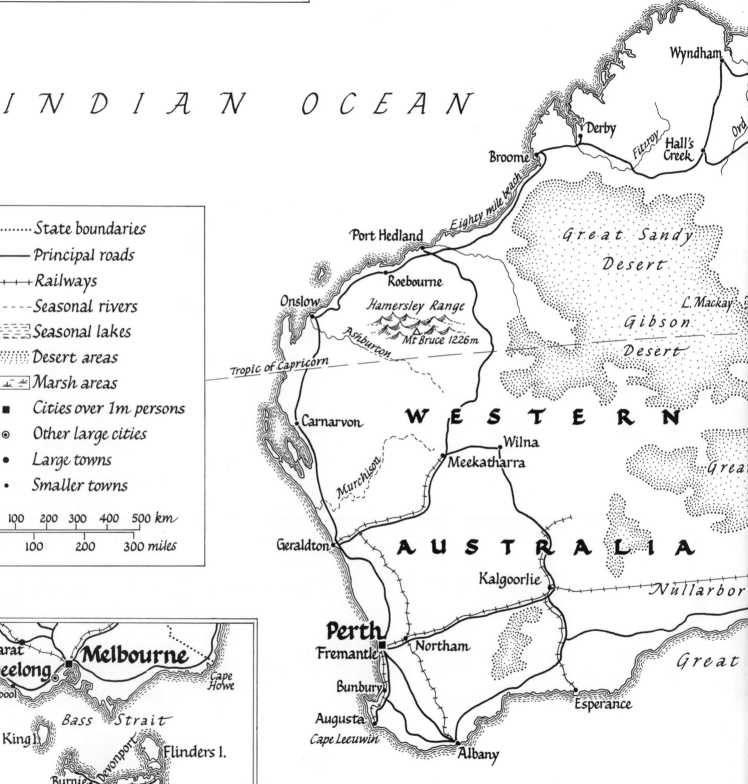

TIMOR SEA

INDIAN OCEAN

Wyndham

Derby

Hall's Creek

Broome

Eighty mile beach

Port Hedland

Great Sandy Desert

Roebourne

Onslow

Hamersley Range

L. Mackay

Gibson Desert

Mt Bruce 1226m

Ashburton

Tropic of Capricorn

Carnarvon

WESTERN

Murchison

Wilna

Meekatharra

Great

Geraldton

AUSTRALIA

Kalgoorlie

Nullarbor

Perth

Fremantle

Northam

Great

Bunbury

Esperance

Augusta

Cape Leeuwin

Albany

SOUTHERN

Legend

··········	State boundaries
——	Principal roads
++++	Railways
- - -	Seasonal rivers
▦	Seasonal lakes
▦	Desert areas
☀	Marsh areas
■	Cities over 1m persons
⊙	Other large cities
•	Large towns
·	Smaller towns

0 100 200 300 400 500 km

0 100 200 300 miles

Ballarat

Geelong

Melbourne

Warrnambool

Cape Howe

Bass Strait

King I.

Flinders I.

Devonport

Burnie

Launceston

TASMANIA

Queenstown

Hobart

(on same scale)

6

ORIGINS

Island or Continent?

1, 2. Miles from nowhere is the impression given by these rounded giants rising from the desert floor. The Olgas, as they are known, are conglomerate protuberances, rich in iron which gives redness to their skin. Mt. Olga, itself, is higher than Ayers Rock 20 miles away. It lifts some 1800 feet into the burning air. To the Aborigines the Olgas are Kata Tjuta, the field of many heads. The Olgas, like Ayers Rock, give shape to the flatland in the south-western corner of the Northern Territory.

3. Ayers Rock, best known stone in the world, is a two-mile-long, 1000-foot-high slab of sandstone. Tourists flock to the monolith, spellbound by the naked mountain, captivated by the colours thrown out at dawn and dusk in slanting sunlight. Aborigines worshipped the rock, called it Uluru, centre of the world, home of the living and the dead. (pp. 12-13)

4. The Great Barrier Reef off Queensland's east coast is, like Ayers Rock, one of Australia's star tourist attractions. The biggest living thing in the world, this multi-biogenic organism contains some 400 different kinds of coral, 1500 species of fish, 4000 types of mollusc, and a seemingly endless variety of sea urchins, starfish, crabs, shrimps and sponges. (pp. 14-15)

5. Where once an ancient forest stood, now all that remains are these fossilised relics. The Pinnacles, limestone moulds of fossil trees, cast long shadows down Nambung National Park, 160 miles north of Perth. They, too, are part of the Aborigine Dreamtime. (pp. 16-17)

Australia, island or continent, is a question sometimes asked. The answer is not simple. With its nearly three million square miles of fascinating and richly varied territory that ranges from the high, permanently snow-covered peak of Mt. Kosciusko to the parched and burning deserts of the arid heartland, seldom touched by rain, Australia is both.

Geographically Australia is classified as a continent. Its vast continuous landmass places it alongside Europe, Asia and the Americas in the continental range. Its resources, mineral and agricultural, its ability to provide for its own basic needs, are on a continental scale. The way it has touched the rest of the world through its people, their talents, their attitudes, even their form of speech, is internationally wide-ranging, continental in every degree.

Yet Australia is also an island, a body of land surrounded by water, washed by the waves of six seas. Planted between the Pacific and Indian Oceans, its oddly circular shape has shorelines that run northward into the Timor Sea, the Arafura Sea and, to the east, the Coral Sea. Further south is the Tasman. Australia's outline would be circular, the classic island shape, if it were not for two great missing pieces that look as if they might have been removed in two enormous bites. In the south is the Great Australian Bight, in the north the Gulf of Carpentaria.

Once, about one hundred and thirty-five million years ago, according to Alfred Wagener's theory of continental drift, Australia was part of the giant mother landmass called Panagea. Panagea was ripped apart by huge forces, enormous sheets of energy beneath the surface of the earth, to form the world as we know it today. The propelling forces, sea-floor spreading, plate tectonics, slowly divided ancient Panagea into two large sections floating slowly, unremittingly apart. The southern of these was Gondwanaland, which contained Australia.

As the millions of years passed, these massive multi-continents, with names that seem to belong to Hobbit country, separated further. Australia moved away from its neighbours, slid outward into the Pacific seas. The rounded gap to the south, the Great Australian Bight, was where it broke away from Antarctica. The smaller gap in the north, the Gulf of Carpentaria, is where New Guinea once nestled against the Australian Northern Territory.

As Australia became isolated, some hundred million years ago, it took with it living and fossil evidence that link it to the motherland, old Gondwanaland of the past. In India there are huge geological basins containing fossils of reptiles — lizards, tortoises, crocodiles — so similar to what has been found in Australia that there is little doubt they were both part of a landscape shared in the geological period known as the Permian. The Permian was a time of warm dry climates ideal for the preservation of the bones, scales, teeth, even the droppings, of creatures that inhabited the land.

Further evidence comes from the massive, frozen slab of land to the south known as Antarctica. There lie coal-beds and other structural similarities it shares with Australia. Very few geologists these days deny Wagener's theory of continental drift: there is too much to support it. And there are many who are convinced that the process is far from over. There is no reason to believe, they say, that the landmasses have stopped moving. The giant plates that form the crust of the earth still grind against each other. Earthquakes bombard the land, volcanoes gush along well-known fracture zones, and there is no reason to expect them to stop.

On this basis a projected map of the earth has been worked out on computers. If the drift of continents continues at the same rate as in the

6. One of Australia's best known symbols, the gentle kangaroo, an inhabitant of the country since before the Aborigine came. They ranged in size from tiny rat-kangaroos to the now-extinct procoptodon, which stood some ten feet tall. Kangaroos are marsupials; they nurture their young in an external pouch from an almost embryonic stage. A kangaroo is present on the Australian coat of arms opposite an emu, the giant flightless bird. Both are representatives of a land separated early, in geological time, from the rest of the planet's landmass.

7. *Another Australian symbol: the farm-house beneath the spreading gum tree. However new, however run-down, man's dwellings have measured his progress through the land. Some are of wood, others of stone, almost all have the ubiquitous corrugated iron roof, painted red, peeling in the unrelenting sun. Here, at Alice Springs, an old cart stands before the house, elsewhere it might be a truck with four-wheel drive. Both are part of Australia, both represent man's struggle to draw sustenance from a hard, at times merciless, land.*

8, 9. From tidal flats and coastal lakes like this in Western Australia the country produces nearly seven million tons of salt a year. That's a lot of pinches. Scanty rainfall and a high rate of evaporation make salt-harvesting cheap. Sea water is channelled into concentrating ponds where it is absorbed by the power of the sun. Salt concentration rises. When the time is right, the pond is drained. Finally, sparkling white crystals of pure salt are formed, taken away and packaged. Then the cycle is repeated. With the fire from the sun, the richness of the sea, the process goes on endlessly.

10. Meandering like huge sullen serpents through miles of flat green-clad countryside, many of Australia's rivers flow sluggishly down to the sea. This in the Cairns region is a typical river in geological old age. It is no longer young, streaming down valleys or gorges, carving out its bed. It wanders peacefully from side to side, often leaving cut-off bends known a billabongs (from 'billa', the Aborigine word for water.)

11. Australia has few great rivers compared to its landmass. The south-east corner is where most of them run. The Murray, the longest, travels through 1600 miles of New South Wales, Victoria and South Australia. The country's other large drainers, the Murrumbidgee, the Lachlan and the Darling, all work the same part of the land. Elsewhere, coastal rivers are short and swift or meander like the one above, while the Dry Heart has few permanent watercourses.

past, in fifty million years' time Australia will have moved so far that the Equator, now some twelve degrees to the north, will cut through the centre of the country, pass through the oasis town of Alice Springs.

As Australia moved on its isolated way, it carried ancient forms of plant and animal life that have remained preserved down the corridors of time. The best known of these are the marsupials and the monotremes, the two most primitive forms of living mammals.

Marsupials are a group of creatures that carry their young in pouches, in a kiddie-carrier that's built in. The most familiar marsupial of all is the great bounding kangaroo, almost the Australian national symbol. The young are born in what is close to a foetal state, tiny, unformed, struggling for life. They crawl up their mother's belly seeking the nipple in the pouch and there they remain until they are fully formed. Their development is remarkable, as is their instinct to survive.

To make the long climb up to the safety of Mama's pouch, the nascent creature develops its forelimbs before its hind limbs, enabling it to drag its way toward the teat that will keep it alive. The teat itself is designed to feed the new-born life — it has special muscles that inject milk into the baby's mouth.

Even lower down on the mammalian scale are the monotremes, the mammals that actually lay eggs. The name monotreme means a single passage. The animals bear that name because, like their reptile ancestors and the birds, they have a single backside exit for both reproductive and excretory business. The eggs they lay are usually soft-shelled, covered by a sort of leathery skin. Some take their young into a pouch after the eggs have hatched like their marsupial cousins.

The curious duck-billed platypus and the other surviving monotreme, the spiny ant-eater, are the most primitive mammals that exist in the world today. Both these living fossils have protruding muzzles that are dark and look as if they've been fashioned out of a soft but durable plastic. As its name implies, the duck-billed platypus has a shovel-shaped, duck-shaped 'snorer', to use an Australian word for nose, which it uses to scoop the snails and shrimps it feeds on out of riverbank mud.

The spiny ant-eater's snorer is a long tubular structure used for digging ants out of their nests, poking into the corridors of ant-hills and sucking out the inhabitants. It has claws to help it break down ant-fortresses, some of which are as hard as iron. The platypus, to equip it for its chosen life-style, has webbed feet, all the better to swim with, to clamber through the mud.

The monotremes have survived only in Australia and New Guinea. Although marsupials are known in other parts of the world, they have flourished in Australia, where they enjoy a range that is not seen in any other country. The reason for this survival, this success, is because they were allowed to live in peace. Australia separated from its sister continents before the three great hunting families of mammals developed, before cats and dogs and pigs came to rule the land.

No native cats have ever been discovered in Australia. Before ancestors of the fleet-footed flesh-eaters, the lions, the tigers, the leopards and cheetah, began their domination of the planet, Australia had broken its links. Nor have any native pigs ever been seen on Australia's soil. They weren't there to root out nests and eggs, to eat the young of the spiny anteaters or the duck-billed platypus, as they did elsewhere on the earth. The only dog that is native to Australia is the dingo, thought to have been brought to the country by early Aborigines thousands of years ago, but certainly long after the split from Gondwanaland.

12. Wave Rock, nearly 200 miles north of Perth, Western Australia. It is the perfect wave in multicoloured sand-stone, part of a formation two billion years old. Carved by wind and sand into a billowing breaker about to fall, Wave Rock is part of a wildlife sanctuary that includes other weather-formed rock sculptures intriguingly named Hippo's Yawn and The Humps. Nearby are the vast Western Australian wheatfields with their own sweeping waves of golden grain.

So, in many ways, continental Australia is an island drifting in space and time, a segment of the past that gives us an idea of what the world was like over a hundred million years ago. Without it we might never have come to know that other Australian symbol, the koala, sometimes called the koala bear although not related to bears at all. Similarly, another marsupial found in Australia, the flying squirrel, is not a squirrel and cannot fly. This small, squirrel-like creature, with a bushy tail, has large folds of skin between the back and front legs on either side which enable it to glide.

There are some one hundred and seventy species of Australian marsupials that burrow, run, hop or glide, and live at all levels, from nests beneath the earth to the tops of the highest trees. All are specialised, some so intelligently developed, like the bandycoots, a group of rat-like creatures, that the pouch in which they keep their young faces backwards so that when Mama is busy digging up the insects the family lives on, the dirt doesn't get into baby's eyes.

And they are, by and large, all gentle animals, making one wonder what the world might have been like if the great flesh-eaters, the hunters in the chain, had not developed as they did. An idle thought, I know, as idle as pondering what else would have been preserved in a fold of time if man had not trodden Australian soil.

The first, the Aborigine, the Native Australian as he or she is known in these days of political correctness, came to the country about forty thousand years ago. They came, as all men are believed to have come, from the north — through Asia and India to the uninhabited lands of the southern hemisphere. They are believed to have followed game, seeking fresh fields, pastures new. Some theories assume the Australian Aborigines crossed land bridges that no longer exist; others suggest that they travelled by canoe, moving from dot to dot on distant horizons until the reached the Cape York Peninsula — less than a hundred miles from the New Guinea shore. Once safely on land, the country was theirs. No competition existed.

Competition came however, in later waves of migrants, each time with more deadly intensity. The original settlers were forced to the south, to Tasmania, where they remained until the white man, the most brutal of all, annihilated them.

The white man did his best to annihilate the Aborigines who lived in mainland Australia. The blackfellow, as he was known, was common game to the white man's gun. Some believed that the Aborigine was no more than a pest, getting in the way of colonial development, that to shoot them down was the same as shooting a wild dingo or any other nuisance in the land. And, although every governor of Australia received instructions from the British Crown that the natives must not be molested in their way of life, they were pushed aside as the white man's colony grew, and their lifestyle was almost destroyed.

They died, as the South American Indians died, through disease and wastage, because new livestock, the sheep and cattle brought by this wave of settlers, took over the land once held by the kangaroo, the wallaby, the small marsupial animals on which the Aborigines depended to keep themselves alive. But, most of all, the black men died because their Songlines were taken from them. Songlines, those tribal canons passed down through the generations from voice to voice, that gave direction, belief and meaning to the Aborigines' semi-nomadic ways, were dislocated by the coming of the European. With the guidelines gone, the Aborigines no longer had a creed to live by. They became pathetic imitators of the men from overseas, the new masters of their universe. In the end they were almost wiped out.

So, for Australia, history turned again. The massive chunk of

Gondwanaland no longer floated free. Once more it was affected by what occurred in other lands. It would never be an island again, never in quite the same way.

In later chapters we will return to look at these introductory themes in greater detail. Now we must move on, examine the shape of Australia as it is today. Broadly speaking there are three great categories: the Dry Heart, the Outback and the Civilised Rim. Let us begin in the centre and move outwards.

The Dry Heart

Almost in the centre of Australia is a town called Alice Springs. It is a cross-roads town, a border town close to the southern edge of the Northern Territory, lifted a little above the surrounding heat by the Macdonnell Ranges. From Alice Springs, whichever way you look, there is nothing but desert all around. The Gibson Desert, the Sandy Desert, the Great Victoria Desert, the Simpson Desert, they stretch for miles. As Australia itself is surrounded by sea, its heart is surrounded by sand.

Two million of Australia's three million square miles are classified as desert of one kind or another. By definition a desert is a place that receives less than ten inches of rainfall, or any other form of precipitation, per year. But all deserts are not purely sand, do not resemble the ranges of dunes that Peter O'Toole staggered over, playing Lawrence of Arabia on the cinema screen. Many are sheets of bare rock carved by wind and rain into stony moonscapes that seem hostile to every form of life. Rain, at times, comes bucketing down to pour off the exposed rock surface that lies crumbling in the sun, unprotected by any plant life. The rushing water collects loose stones and sand to deposit at the mouth of the gully it cuts, each time deeper and deeper.

Soon the water sinks into the alluvial fan it has formed at the gully-mouth and disappears. Then the winds take over. As they rise they pick up fine sand, small stones, and like buzz-saws shear into the landscape. Sometimes the incisions they make are at angles to the deep rain-gullies and so they carve, the rain and the wind, patterns in the surface of the earth, reducing it, turning it into rubble, making a desert. This, of course, takes time. It takes thousands, millions of years. But then time, in geological terms, is something this planet has not yet been short of.

Australia has a wide range of desert country. In the central west the Gibson and the Sandy Deserts have sand dunes and hard rocky faces. It is hard to imagine life in such aridity, on such an unwelcoming section of land. But it exists, however uncertainly; there are creatures even here who have learned how to survive. They are tiny and tough, the ones that persist, such as the ants that have among the members of the nest some that act as food stores. Their abdomens swell as they take in honey from the rest of the colony. They store it and when times get tough, when there is no moisture anywhere else, it is recycled to keep the rest of the tribe alive. They live, as do other survivors of their kind, among the roots of equally tough tussock grass or spinifex, which forms small resistant barriers at the feet of dunes where a little moisture might trickle down, where the wind is less severe.

In this section of desert Australia, in the driest corner of the country's heart, is one of its most famous landmarks — Ayers Rock, the largest single rock in the entire world. This oval-shaped giant is some four miles long, nearly one and a half wide and almost a fifth of a mile high. It rises about two hundred miles south-west of Alice Springs as the crow flies —

not that a crow would be silly enough to attempt such a flight in the heat. Ayers Rock, when it catches rain, is a massive red monster, pockmarked, warts and all, lying in a field of dream-like brilliance, as the desert blooms. It really does. Seeds that may have been lying in wait for a year or more, that may have taken in a little moisture but need more before full germination takes place, will suddenly shoot forth their colours. Salt bushes that have been black, looked dead, become verdant and vital. The native mulga bush, Australian acacia, whose leaves have browned and dried, will turn green again, lift its head, begin to grow afresh; its yellow or white flowers will bud and blossom. The power of the rain to transform the desert's face, to bring out the beauty that lies hidden in the earth, never fails to astonish.

Ayers Rock, with its rain, lifted a little above the sandy floor, is a zone of transition to the second of Australia's three massive areas — the Outback, where man can live and work, where larger animals abound. Unlike the Dry Heart, deserted literally by most forms of life, the Outback, even though it might receive less than ten inches of rainfall a year, seems almost overpopulated, brimming with movement and growth.

The Outback

As its name implies, the Outback is the countryside beyond the cities, the towns, the settlements that inhabit the Civilised Rim. It is cattle country, stock country, the land where mines have been developed, where man has made his mark. The great sweeps of the Outback that circle Australia's dry heartland include a huge semi-circle that runs along the northern coast and some way down to the east. It consists of eucalyptus forests and tussocky, grassy flatlands. Another section covers Australia's south-eastern corner; there is more to the west of the Great Australian Bight; there are pockets in other corners of the land.

This is the classic Australian landscape where kangaroos and koalas dwell, where cockatoos screech their unoiled cries, where Sydney Nolan painted his barren landscapes, where Ned Kelly and his infamous outlaws rode roughshod over the land. That is, if the legends are to be believed, if the gilt of romance is overlaid thickly enough. Such legends have grown because the Outback, like America's Wild West, is hard country to live in, hard country in which to survive, and always it seems that where life is hard legends are born, given voice, so that those who tell them may share in the glory, may become part of the tale itself.

Before man came with his gilded tongue, the Outback belonged to

Shipping detained in Hobson's Bay, Williamstown, for Captain Phillip, 1852

more modest creatures. They had not been hunted for their flesh, they were non-aggressive in their own behaviour. Living on leaves and fruit, on flowers and twigs, they were the hippies of their time. Some of their peacefulness, their ability to survive the harshness of their climate, is reflected in the names the Aborigines gave them. Koala comes from the original native *koolah*, it means: the animal that does not drink.

Other Outback inhabitants developed other ways of living through the heat, the long dry periods when no rain fell. There is, for example, a fat-tailed mouse that stores food in the form of fat in that part of its anatomy. Some tiny marsupial mice don't drink at all, but get their moisture from the plants and seeds they eat, however tough and dry their diet may seem. The wombat, another Australian marsupial with an other-world name, about the size of the koala, digs long underground burrows to escape from the heat. In its tunnel, sometimes more than ten feet long, this rat-like, pig-like, hairy creature, lies quietly away from the furnace of the day to emerge at night.

Many desert animals are the same. They come out from their hiding places in the evening to eat, explore, mate and wander for an hour or two, often returning to their caves when desert temperatures plummet during the night. In the early morning they poke their noses once more into the outside world when the air is fresh, the sun not yet hot, to enjoy a few more hours in the hard cycle of their lives.

I knew a man in Sydney who lived above the zoo on the far side of the harbour. The Sydney Zoo, one of the best kept, most fascinating in the world, came to life in the early morning. Each day my friend walked down through the maze of chirping, screeching, buzzing life to catch the ferry that took him to the far side of the water, to the city where he worked. In the evening, after a day of telephones and meetings, of short tempers and long lunches, he returned and climbed back up the hill through the animal-packed piece of land. It was a little calmer in the evening, some of the early energy was dimmed but, in his opinion, these were the two most valuable stretches of his day. To see the vitality all around him made him realise that there was more to life that what the glass-walled city contained.

Australia's best-known animal is the long-tailed kangaroo. With its back legs developed for jumping, a form of locomotion that computers indicate is highly energy-saving, it bounds from one clump of grass to another. There are several sizes, colours and even shapes of kangaroo but the largest, up to nine feet from tip of tail to top of head, is the Sooty. I once drove from Melbourne to Mt. Isa, a distance of almost three thousand miles, and along the way, in fields, beneath the ubiquitous gum tree, were many kangaroos. I remember being taken by their peacefulness, their tranquillity, as we went past, churning up clouds of thick red dust from the rough country roads. They looked like gentle maiden aunts as they reposed among the tussocky grasses, their little forearms crossed over their chests, their eyes watching us carefully, making sure we were being good.

But what impressed me more on that long, dry drive was the wealth of birdlife. There were flocks of pink and grey galahs, a smallish member of the cockatoo family that squawks and shrieks with such intensity that its name has passed into the Australian tongue. 'Don't be a galah,' they'll say. 'Don't be a bloody fool.' Other bigger cockatoos, white and black, with crests that rise like colonial governors' helmets, also filled the air with their screaming, especially in the early morning in some small cowboy town where they circled seeking water, a cattle trough, an uncovered tank, anywhere to get a drink. I've known other Australians, in similar towns, to shout their demands as loudly, but it wasn't water they were looking for.

All these creatures of the Outback depend on the coming of the rains, the Wet, as it's known locally, the tail-end of the monsoon that sweeps across the dry, red landscape, turning it, however briefly, into a form of paradise. This occurs, especially in the northern segment, in the summer. Then, however sparse the annual supply of rain might be, it comes at once, swooping over the landscape, turning dry stream beds into torrents, filling wells and waterholes, lagoons and billabongs to the brim. Suddenly the sky can seem full of white, heavy-chested, long-billed pelicans as they take off, disturbed, from a waterhole where they have been feeding on the new life brought into being by the Wet.

Australian birdlife includes some of the largest species on the planet. The emu, second only to the ostrich in size, is flightless now, but runs very fast indeed. I once measured the speed of one that insisted on racing ahead on the same narrow strip of roadway as my jeep. It reached forty miles an hour before it dived off into the shrubbery. But once, a long time ago, the emu, as did its Australian cousin the cassowary, flew from island to island to reach the Australian shore. The great landmass may have been floating away with its cargo of pre-hunting fauna, but that did not prevent the birds of the air from reaching it. Some, like the emu, then lost their ability to fly. There was no need for it anymore; they were happy, scratching, where they were.

The rain that comes briefly to the Outback falls more steadily on the Civilised Rim, making it hospitable to both animal and man. This has not been to the animals' advantage. Man, in his need and greed, has occupied, altered, transformed this part of old Gondwanaland, making it his own.

The Civilised Rim

Vast forests, of one kind or another, separate the Civilised Rim from the rest of Australia. In the north these forests are tropical. To the south they are temperate, Mediterranean in their climate. Throughout all the wooded areas is found the famous Australian gum tree, the blue gum, the eucalyptus. Koalas sometimes spend their entire life in gum trees, seldom touching the ground. The young leaves and the bark provide them with food and moisture as well as somewhere to nest, breed and take care of their offspring. Where rainfall is less plentiful, the gums share their environment with tough grasses and thorny shrubs. In wetter places they grow with birch and pine and the giant fern trees which can reach eighty feet in height.

Rainfall in Australia is largely controlled by the Great Dividing Range, a huge chain of mountains, of various origins and character, that runs down the east coast of Australia from Cape York in the north to the state of Victoria in the south, where they merge into Australian Alps. This highland barrier is also the dividing line as far as rainfall is concerned. Wind from the east, the main source of all Australian air currents, is lifted by the mountains and sheds its moisture there. Thus the Great Dividing Range and its neighbouring landscapes pirate the rain before it has much chance to spread further west, resulting in deserts of the country's Dry Heart and the arid marginal areas of the Outback.

But where rain does fall its effect is marked and wonderful. Dense forest cover provides safety, food and nesting places for a spectrum of wildlife that runs from genuine wetland creatures like the brightly-striped gold and black corroboree frog, which lays its eggs in moss along the mountain ranges, to similarly coloured, six-foot-long iguanas that can scramble over hard-scale rock with the speed of a running dog. Goannas,

Dead emu, engraving, 1857

the Australians call them, using a slight corruption of the basic name. You can start a conversation in almost any bar in any part of the country by mentioning the big goanna you saw or the snake you nearly stood on. Everyone has seen a bigger iguana, found a larger snake in their bed, or has heard of someone who's done so. Like fishermen talking about the one that got away, Australians respond to tales of their country's reptiles; it's part of the cowboy, the stockman, the jackeroo or jilleroo, they keep in a corner of their heart.

Jackeroos, and their female counterparts, jilleroos — feminism is not totally absent in Australian cattle country — are the men and women who ride herd, often mile after dry mile, covering the massive land holdings that some possess in the north and south-east of the country. Here farmland is often measured not in square acres but in square miles, the holdings are so vast.

When man came to Australia, first the waves of Aborigines and then those from Europe, it was on the Civilised Rim that they made their homes. There they found, like the wildlife before them, abundant food and water, place to build their nests. Aborigines were semi-nomadic, and moved from place to place within their own area. They, like the white man who followed, were as restricted as the rains by the great mountain wall that ran down the east side of the country. All clung, for many years, to the seaward, fruitful edge.

The first Aborigines came to Australia some forty thousand years ago; the first white man set foot on the land in the sixteenth century. For forty thousand years the Aborigines left the country almost as it was; they brought the first dogs, they altered the ecological balance a little, but they made no major change to the island continent in its minuscule drift between its seas. In little over two hundred years the men from Europe altered the shape of the land beyond recognition — but only where they have been able to, where the elements have let them — on and around the Civilised Rim. The rest remains a desert.

In 1770, James Cook, the renowned English navigator, led a party of Englishmen ashore at Botany Bay on the east coast of Australia, an unknown stretch of the land. He claimed the country in the name of the British Crown, and there was no one to oppose him. The Aborigines, it seems, were won over by gifts, by the sight of the English ships, by the impressiveness of the English guns. Nor were the original inhabitants possessive people. They made no claims, staked out no soil, probably stood in wonder at the overdressed men with their pale skins, funny hats and flags, doing whatever they thought they needed to do in order to take possession of a piece of the planet just because it and they happened to be there, and because no one was objecting.

For seventeen years after Captain Cook and his men from the *Endeavour* performed their ritual of taking-over, Australia remained untouched. The Aborigines continued their own way of life. The gifts they had received would have broken or become faded. Perhaps some were placed on rocks or tree-tops as objects of worship, in the same way as the natives of New Guinea were to worship aircraft not so very long ago. Having witnessed the great birds flown by the white man land and bring forth their cargoes of wealth and beauty, groups of natives attempted to lure the creatures down to their part of the earth. They cleared long strips of land to create mock-runways and built crude aircraft from sticks and branches, the leaves from coconut palms, to act as decoys, in the same way a duck-hunter hopes to bring a flock within range of his gun. They sat in wait for hours, days, weeks, but no birds came down laden with treasures.

13. Another famous Australian character, the koala. With its beady eyes and shiny black nose the koala is known and loved throughout the world. This sleepy creature was called by the Aborigines 'the animal that does not drink'. Tender young eucalyptus bark and leaves provide all the food and drink it needs. Some koalas pass their entire lifetime without their feet ever touching the ground.

The Aborigines, on the other hand, and much to their misfortune, did see the return of the men with pale skins. But whatever it was the Aborigines might have hoped for, they could never have imagined what the British had in mind when they returned.

They brought more gifts, beads and ribbons were handed out, they offered wine to taste and fired their rifles to show the blackfellows who jumped and danced, shouted and brandished their spears on the shore, that they were the new and rightful owners of what was to be a promised land for many in the centuries to come. But Australia was not then designed to be a paradise for the more than seven hundred prisoners the new fleet of English ships carried in their holds.

For the next eighty years and more, some part of the vast landmass or another would serve as a penal colony, a place to which prisoners, male and female, were to be transported. It was distant, remote, over the horizon. And it was believed by many in the English judicial hierarchy that once these misfits in society were removed from English soil they would no longer be a problem to anyone in the British Isles. Out of sight and out of mind was the simple belief that set Australia on the path to what it has become today.

The idea of shipping off the riff-raff was not new. For England, while it held American colonies, transportation of felons not only rid the country of their presence, but provided a relatively constant source of slave labour in the cotton and tobacco plantations of America, mainly in Virginia. This system worked well as far as nearly everyone was concerned. Even for the convicts it must have been better to be sent overseas than hanged for a crime as petty as stealing a loaf of bread.

However, the American Revolution in 1775 put an end to the practice. Americans no longer wanted English outcasts. What is more, they now had an abundant alternative supply of slave labour. While convicts had been exported at the rate of some one thousand a year, African slaves were arriving in America at about fifty times that number. So English judges had to scratch beneath their wigs and think of other places the unwanted might be sent. For a while West Africa was favoured, but the climate there was too unhealthy: not only the convicts but their overseers would perish. South Africa was considered and rejected also, as were Tristan da Cunha and Madagascar. Choice fell upon Australia, and those at the top of English society breathed a sigh of relief. Australia was not only on the far side of the globe, it was almost totally unknown. No criminal would ever escape from there.

On May 13, 1787, a fleet of ships set sail from Portsmouth in the south of England. On board were one thousand and thirty people, seven hundred and thirty-six of them prisoners. These eleven vessels, the First Fleet as they came to be known, sailed for just over eight months before arriving at Australia. They were under the command of Captain Arthur Phillip. He sailed along the coastline Cook had mapped seventeen years earlier and he didn't like what he saw.

Botany Bay, where Cook had landed, was not the lush landscape Phillip had been led to expect. He went ashore, collected water, handed out a few beads and mirrors to the uncertain Aborigines and when the rest of his fleet arrived, he sailed north to Port Jackson. There he decided to found his penal colony. There, where one day the coat-hanger Sydney Harbour Bridge would span the water, where the cockle-shell Sydney Opera House would nestle by the sea, he anchored his fleet, and began to set ashore his cargo of convicts and settlers. In doing so Arthur Phillip broke open the cocoon Australia had lived in since the beginning of geological time.

14-19. Koalas are marsupials that came to Australia when it was linked to other continents that have long since drifted apart. They survived because Australia separated before flesh-eating cats were around to hunt them down, or monkeys to chase them from their trees. Their problem today, however, is that there are too many leaf-munchers and not enough eucalyptus trees. An ecological balance needs to be established between the koalas and their food supply, if only because there seems to be a thriving industry developing in the sale of koala droppings as lucky charms, especially in Japan.

20-22. In a land of unusual wildlife it's reasonable to expect a range of uncommon road signs. These warn against the possibility of running into emus, kangaroos or camels. Others indicate the presence of wombats or possums on Outback highways miles from any settlement. Like all creatures, those in Australia are dazzled by headlights springing out of the dark and attempt, too late, to flee. Life for them is hard enough without the danger of being mown down by a speeding truck.

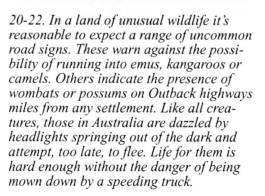

23. Although once closely tied to England, Australia is slowly drifting away. Distances are now measured in kilometres, as this road sign indicates. Traffic, however, still travels on the left-hand side of the road. The Queen, as Queen of Australia, remains the country's titular head. This, too, may alter soon. A referendum will be held to decide if Australia is to become a republic.

24-25. Patterns on a landscape, etchings that will one day give birth to wine. Here, in the Barossa Valley, South Australia, some of the country's finest vineyards produce a quarter of Australia's wine. Originally settled by German Lutherans seeking refuge from persecution in the 1840s, the Barossa Valley slowly became one of the centres of viticulture. For many years Aussie wines were just called 'plonk', but today they are rated amongst the best in the world, although they say that the finest never leave Australia. They're consumed at home.

26. *A giant acacia, the Australian wattle, another national symbol. Here, on Cape York Peninsula. Queensland's most northern tip, Australia's largest lowland rain forest spreads in a dense interweaving of pine, cedar and acacia. Beneath the trees, fern and creeper interlock with flowering shrubs. After rain, the air is rich with moisture, the scent of earth and flowers, a heady confirmation of life and the living.*

27. Monolithic anthills, built up crumb by crumb by the workers of the nest, can reach a height of 25 feet. They can fill open scrubland in Australia's north with their castles, aligned firmly north and south. Such anthills have been called magnetic because they creep toward the poles. The truth is that they are designed to catch maximum sunlight, east and west, keeping their occupants warm.

28. Untouched by the white man until the great explorers opened up the land, the Outback, the desert country, is today a tourist magnet. Tourism represents more than five per cent of Australia's gross domestic product, provides some half a million jobs.

29. Australian wines from the Barossa Valley, Hunter River or Rutherglen have enjoyed enormous success in the past 15 years. Exports today are four times those of the mid-1980s. About 400 million litres are produced each year but only about a tenth is exported.

30-36. Kangaroos have their own specialised mobility — the bounding leap.
With speeds of 30 miles an hour they
spring over fences 10 foot high. No one's
sure why kangaroos leap. Maybe with baby
in a pouch there's less chance of it falling
out if Mama is not running on all four feet.

37. An undulating moonscape (overleaf), the Macdonnell Ranges, stretching east and west near Alice Springs. Among the most ancient mountains on earth, they go back some 400 million years. Beside them, straight as man can make it, runs a desert highway — a slice through time as temporary as today.

SETTLEMENT

Crude Beginnings

There can have been no other moment in the history of mankind when two so completely different races came to share a piece of land under such freakish circumstances. The native population, of course, had no choice in the matter, although there is nothing particularly unusual about that. But they had nothing the white invaders wanted: no gold, no silver, no wealth at all.

Phillip and his men were not drawn by greedy dreams of untold riches. Unlike Hernan Cortés, when he conquered Mexico or Francisco Pizarro, when he marched into Peru, they did not believe that immeasurable treasure lay there for the taking. Nor were they inspired by a spirit of Christian righteousness — the bringing of the word of God to heathen souls. They didn't even want the Aborigines' women; they found them ugly and thought they stank — a remarkable statement from a group of men who had sailed for some two hundred and fifty days under vile conditions.

What the English fleet had come for, nothing more and nothing less, was to dump a cargo of human garbage on a distant, secure shore. Those in charge would watch their prisoners, see that they did not escape, put them to work and, if possible, try and build a colony on the bleak, dry landscape. But these were secondary considerations. First and foremost had been to relieve the pressure on overcrowded English jails and the rotting hulks of prison-ships that hung off the English coast, to remove undesirables, as far away as possible, hoping they'd cause no more trouble.

As for the Aborigines, it is impossible to know what they thought of the huge boats sitting in the splendid (Sydney) harbour, where flat-bedded sandstone lines the shore, slab over slab of golden stone. Or what they imagined when the great vessels put out their creature-craft and the strangely dressed men began to row ashore. Perhaps some of them remembered the gifts given out seventeen years before, perhaps others had heard of the sticks these people carried that exploded and could kill. Perhaps they stood on one leg, as they were known to do, the instep of the lifted leg resting on the knee of the other, like cranes still in the water waiting to see what the day will bring. They had gathered in impressive numbers as the First Fleet arrived. They threw a warning spear or two when the white men stepped ashore. One of the Englishmen fired a shot. Little more violence is recorded. Boxes of beads were opened, ribbons were handed out. The Aborigines came closer, touched and pulled at the Englishmen's clothes; they had never seen anyone so overdressed. A certain natural curiosity was expressed about what lay under the garments until someone opened his trousers and the natives were able to see for themselves that, at least in that department, the newcomers were much like everyone else.

That, however, was the good news. A relatively peaceful landing had been made. What lay ahead was grimmer, much more difficult to manage than the meeting on the shore. The English had arrived with little idea of what awaited them, in complete ignorance of the Australian continent, and with few plans of how they were going to survive. There had been some talk of developing a flax industry, of exporting pine and other timber, but they had not even brought the tools to begin any sort of industry. As they set up their tents, cut into the trees, dug latrines, they were like brightly-dressed vacationers who had arrived for a jolly picnic and now couldn't get away. They were campers, inexperienced, inept and in danger.

The First Fleet carried little livestock; they had dry or salted rations which would see them through the first few months, but in terms of breeding animals they had three cows and two bulls, less than fifty sheep, fewer hogs and a collection of chickens, ducks and turkeys — little future fodder for the just under one thousand people who landed on Australia's coast, not

38. An assemblage of man-made vehicles crouched under the sloping grandeur of Ayers Rock. Insect-like, humans scale Uluru, the Aborigines' sacred stone. Ayers Rock can be ascended in 45 minutes, with a chain to help the climber up. Already the steady procession of tourist-feet has begun to wear a pathway into the surface of the ancient monument.

nearly enough to see them through.

Of course, the convict cargo, being less than decent folk, could be given the most basic of rations, gruel or bread and water, but, even so, they had to be fed. What's more, they had to be taken off the stinking ships, out of the bilge-infested holds, given somewhere to sleep on the land. And this was when Arthur Phillip's real troubles began.

Once ashore, the convicts tried to escape, and succeeded. A number fled down the coast where they made contact with a French boat that had sailed in behind the English. But the French didn't want them either and they were finally returned to what was, by then, called Sydney Cove. But that was only the beginning of what was to be decades of disorder. The day enough rough huts had been constructed to bring the female convicts ashore, some dressed in frocks or skirts and blouses, others in wheat and tapioca sacks, Sydney saw its first real riot. The weather broke, a violent thunderstorm lashed the newly-founded camp, fires were put out, tents blown into water-filled ditches, prisoners ran free and together with drunken sailors chased the women, raping them when they could — it must have been a spectacle worthy of a Fellini film. One wonders what might have passed through the minds of any Aborigines watching the unruly scene. Perhaps it made them realise that the white men were not gods at all.

The Native Australians

It has become almost impossible to know what the Aborigines thought of the white men and their coming to the land that had been theirs, practically unmolested, for thousands upon thousands of years. They recorded nothing in writing. They painted on walls, on bark, on their own bodies, but the meanings carried by the paintings are less than clear. It seems that they believed in life after death, some Creator of all living things. Bodies were placed in trees on various occasions, at times on platforms built above the earth. Great importance was given to the undoubted powers of thunder and lighting, forces that split the skies. It is said that they thought that daylight came when the morning star was blown into the heavens by almost constant wind from the east. The land and its parts, the mountains, valleys, rivers that sometimes ran, sometimes were nothing but dry beds of sand, seemed to be part of their belief in totemism, their belief that some greater force gave shape, even life itself, to their family, to their tribe.

They performed circumcision, both male and female, in rites of initiation. They had complicated marriage bonds within a family's branches. It is recorded that the most suitable mate for a man old enough to marry — the men married much older than the women — was his mother's mother's brother's daughter's daughter, which sounds like a cousin quite well removed. Incest, however, was taboo and was often regarded as a cause of death, though how the death came about, by an enraged father or the hand of some irate god, has never been recorded, and is beyond our knowledge now.

So as the east wind tore the invaders' houses down, as the lightning illuminated the riotous scene, it is fascinating to ponder what the Aborigines thought as they crouched by their gum trees staring. All the elements of ritualism were being carried out on the muddy soil. God in the heavens was present. The east wind blew. It is said that the Aborigines themselves performed totemic dances, barking or grunting or crying-out in the voice of the totem-beast they celebrated. The frenzy often ended in public coupling. And on that stormy night, before their very eyes, the white men, who had come with their god-like machines, were tearing off their coloured clothing and doing exactly that. Perhaps the Aborigines wondered what beast the invaders had brought to their peaceful land.

However, what they thought we will never know because not only did they fail to write anything about themselves, the invaders also recorded little about the natives they displaced. The convicts, obviously, had less contact at first with the Australian natives, and few of them would have been either interested or capable of taking anthropological notes. The marines guarding the prisoners and most of the others who sailed in on the First Fleet had little interest in anything apart from surviving and finally going home.

The most revealing indication of the white man's attitude toward the black was the term used to describe the Aborigine. They were referred to as 'hordes', that is to say, groups of nomads who moved about without apparent destination. No effort was made to discover tribal differences, to put them into categories according to the area in which they lived. They moved, but also they remained; they had their territories, different languages, and obviously different customs and beliefs. Some of the richness of their lifestyle was unearthed later, some of it is painstakingly being discovered today, but when the English first arrived they spent more time describing the animal and plant life than they did the race that had kept the balance of nature for so many thousands of years.

The Aborigines were 'legally protected' — whatever that was supposed to mean when it was drafted back in London by people with no idea of Aboriginal lifestyle. They were not to be molested, instructions from the British Crown decreed, but the question of how that could be avoided, when their land was being usurped, was carefully avoided. The simple truth is that they were looked upon as a nuisance — ill-armed, unorganised and, like other 'wildlife' on the new horizon, to be controlled. They had skills, however, that were quite valuable as far as the English were concerned. Their ability to trace the passage of either animal or man over the arid landscape became legendary. All their lives, generation after generation, they had hunted with spears, stones and boomerangs, all of which meant that the

Station life in New South Wales, 1883

hunter had to be within throwing distance if he had any chance at all. The Aborigine had learned to track quietly, without being seen, following every little sign he saw and knowing what it meant. Local trackers were kept handy should any convict escape . And like good hound-dogs they were rewarded when they brought their trophies back, given a little tobacco or sugar or even a jar of rum.

It seemed to became a part of their way of life, move into their culture. I worked as a geologist, for a while, in the Queensland Outback. From time to time an Aborigine would appear beside a track, from beneath a tree, usually wearing cattleman's clothes: hard trousers, a shirt, a large hat. He always asked for tobacco. He always called me 'boss'. He was always an isolated individual, alone on his drifting island-continent, holding out his hand, watching.

His ancestors would have watched the performance of the English the day after the women convicts were brought ashore. In a formal ceremony, Governor Phillip, as he then was, harangued the convicts and issued orders that would see men shot if they attempted anything like it again. He also warned the assembled newcomers that equal punishment would be dealt out to anyone who stole livestock. On it the future of the colony and their immediate survival depended. It was the only real wealth they had.

Hard Times

Governor Phillip meant what he said. He hanged convicts for stealing provisions, and on one occasion, six marines. If he was harsh, he needed to be. The settlers' first attempts to grow crops on their newly-taken land were little short of disastrous. The soil was dry and unrewarding, the climate virtually unknown; there weren't even any Aboriginal planters whose expertise could be called on. They were a moving people and probably knew the futility of expecting to survive on what grew in that red, dusty ground.

By the time the English had learned something of the soil, where the best places were, how and when to plant, they had used all the grain available. When crops flourished, their seed had to be saved for future planting, not used as food, and starvation prowled around the colony waiting to take its toll. For five years the colony survived, thin, undernourished, unassembled, but survive it did. Fish in the rocky waters of Sydney harbour were plentiful and although they were not rated highly on an Englishman's diet in those days, they were a life-saving source of protein. And the Australian damper was born. A damper is made from flour and water, with a pinch of salt if it is available, kneaded and flattened into a cake no more than an inch or two thick. It is placed in an open fire, sometimes on a shovel, sometimes on the hot earth, and ashes are dumped on top of it. After half an hour the crisp, ash-covered biscuit is dusted off and eaten. The English didn't rate *them* highly either. I've eaten them in Queensland and I know exactly how they felt.

As well as learning how to use the land, the colonists learned how to build on it. And learn, they had to. The First Fleet had been hurried off so quickly, so urgent was the rush to get transport-sentenced criminals away from society's eyes, it arrived with a paltry number of saws and axes and few men who knew how to use them. A bricklayer had to be found among the convicts. Few of the convicts knew how to work. Some were old or crippled or incapable of learning a basic task, others had so little inclination to build a Fortress Australia that they contributed almost nothing. And the marines, the sailors, those who came in command, were occupied most of the time seeing that the convicts did not escape. Above all, everyone was hungry, stunned by lack of food.

If the arrival of the English in Australia and the confrontation of the Aboriginal race was a bizarre moment in mankind's history, the ill-assorted collection of would-be colonists that arrived on the Australian shore must be one of the most extraordinary ever recorded. As a group they were neither fleeing persecution nor seeking a promised land; they had little in common and nothing, apart from hardship, to share. The convicts had committed individual crimes and had received separate sentences; the marines had joined-up for reasons of their own; the officers had been given a job to do. There was no zeal, no flag to fly, nothing that resembled a mission or a crusade. That the ill-formed colony did not simply disappear, disintegrate or consume itself says something about the human spirit, a spirit that still has a place in many Australian hearts. They don't, very often, cave in.

Relief, for Governor Phillip and his riven society, came in two waves. The first was on the ship he sent to Cape Town to buy emergency supplies. It returned safely with flour and grain in 1789. Seed was planted in Parramatta, now a Sydney suburb, with promising results, but still food stocks were dangerously low. In 1790 the first ship out of England that the newcomers were to see since their arrival sailed into the harbour, carrying letters from loved ones, food, and some two hundred women prisoners. This was to be the pattern for years to come. Ships would arrive at Sydney with boxes full of loving messages from families left behind, with equipment and, at times, a change of guard. They brought food supplies and, almost always, a cargo of living souls that nobody wanted, not in Australia nor in England, whence they had been disposed. Wave after wave of prisoners, some sick, some dying, some already dead, were landed with other supplies. They were cargoes with little hope, no sense of future.

Or so it must have seemed. Especially when they stared at the shabby uniforms their guards had been reduced to wearing, at the ill-made timber-and-daub shelters they would be forced to live in. Their hearts must have sunk even further when they were put to work, undernourished and unskilled, as they saw their fellow prisoners fall and die beneath the weight of timber they were made to carry. Above was a sky of endless blue out of which beat an unrelenting sun. Around them, beyond the faces of their fellow prisoners, the men who guarded them, gaunt as skeletons for lack of food, were the Aborigines. Relatively untouched in those early years by the white man's coming, not yet decimated by syphilis, tuberculosis or rum, the Aborigines watched, their dark eyes unreadable, their heavy-ridged faces stiff with contempt. They were superior to the convicts, and both sides knew it. To the Aborigines it was no more than their birthright — they owned the land, or so they still believed. To the convicts it would have only added to their despair, fired a sullen hatred that one day would break open and lash out.

This was arid land for any hope to grow on, any dream to flourish. Yet the spirit overcame the flesh. By 1792 the first corner in Australia's colonial history had been turned. Crops were increasing steadily; almost enough food was being produced; brick buildings gave an aspect of permanence to the sprawling scene. And, most significantly of all, the first transported convicts had served enough of their time to be granted land to call their own. Some emancipists, as such men were known, began to feed themselves and their families — they had married convict women and were producing children — some of the first white Australians to be born Down Under.

Captain William Bligh, an early governor of the Australian colony known then as New South Wales

Bligh and The Rum Corps

Other land grants were being made. A recently-arrived New South Wales Corps, whose duties included administration and fighting off the French if necessary, was treated liberally. Twenty-five acres of land was available for any soldier who cared to apply. Officers could obtain grants of one hundred acres plus ten convicts to work it as virtual slave labour. Land development began to spread, move away from the coast and the rich fields of Parramatta, and most of the development was controlled by the increasingly powerful New South Wales Corps. Or the Rum Corps, as they came to be called, because they took charge of that commodity too.

As tobacco and drugs are coinage in jails throughout the world today, rum was cash in the early days of settlement in Australia. And the Rum Corps regulated every drop that was imported, as they regulated boots and shovels, carpenters' tools and cloth; everything that landed went through their hands. They were the Mafia of their time. Through control of imports and control of land, these men who held open power — few government officials dared oppose them — made the country much their own. Rum Corps farmers paid less for implements or supplies than the prices they charged the emancipist landsmen. Each time a new batch of convicts arrived, the men of the Rum Corps selected those with skills to work on their own expanding properties. Grasping and often brutal, they bred an even more bitter climate of resentment and greed.

Finally, in an attempt to curtail their excesses, by then well-known in London, William Bligh, the ill-fated captain of the famous *Bounty*, was sent out to govern the colony, still known as New South Wales. Bligh's luck did not improve in Australia; he had another mutiny to deal with. This time it was not his crew that rebelled because both officers and men wanted to remain with the women of Tahiti. In New South Wales those who rose up against him were the leaders of the Rum Corps, who objected to his interference with their monopolies, especially their control of practically all the spirits the colony drank.

When Bligh arrested John Macarthur, the Corps ex-paymaster and high chieftain of most of its schemes, he was thrown in jail himself. The Rum Corps, having got rid of the new governor in less than eighteen months, ruled the colony for the next two years. Such was their power that even when they were finally deposed, none was severely punished. Few received more than a token wrist-slap; none had their properties taken away.

Bligh himself escaped, but never returned to his post as governor. That was the end of him, he never saw service again. In turn the Rum Corps was disbanded on orders from London. It was replaced by a regular regiment, the 73rd Highlanders, whose commander, Lachlan Macquarie, a determined Scottish empire-builder, was appointed the colony's governor. Under his guidance it grew from a penal settlement into a land where a man might be free.

Macquarie's New Order

Lachlan Macquarie was forty-nine when he took over the position of Governor of New South Wales on the first day of January, 1810. He had been a soldier all his life. At fifteen he left his home in Argyll and went to Canada to join the army there. He fought in India and in Ceylon, saw service in Egypt, and when he was dispatched to Australia, it was with the light of a new campaign in his military eye.

Macquarie had a boxer's face, heavy-fleshed and crumpled, with a nose that looked as if it had been broken and a puffiness around the eyes. And he was a man with an undoubted mission — to knock the colony into shape. He began by attacking the rum trade, the cash-flow New South Wales relied on. A duty was imposed on all spirits, making drinking more expensive. In some ways this succeeded, in others it merely put alcoholics more deeply into debt. Public houses were closed on Sundays and the convicts went to church instead. But his attitude towards the convicts contained more than merely missionary zeal; he treated them more generously than many who had held his post before.

Macquarie realised that if the country had a real future, something that went beyond the harvesting of next year's crops or the landing of the next cargo of misfits that nobody really wanted, it lay in developing the landscape. He believed in emancipation, in giving a man who had served his time the chance to husband the land. To his military eye this was promotion, elevation from the ranks to an officer of the terrain.

And convicts kept arriving in ever-increasing numbers. After the Napoleonic wars, when they were no longer any use as cannon-fodder, they poured into Australia, sometimes as many as three thousand a year. Macquarie handled the inflow well. He put those who were capable to work on constructing public buildings, on establishing in permanent terms the city of Sydney, on making the colony scratched out on the shore into a lasting settlement. This, he was convinced, was another of his campaign tasks.

Macquarie must have been dismayed by the enormity of the work that needed to be done when he first set eyes on Sydney, eyes that had seen some of the greatest and most delicate architecture in the world, from the sturdy granite buildings of his own Argyll to the stately temples in India and Ceylon. However, he set about the task, as an experienced military man

Emigrants bound for Sydney, The Illustrated London News, April 13, 1844

would, by using what he had to hand. There was precious little. There were no architects among the free-men who walked Sydney's shabby streets; there were no master-builders. However, among the convicts there was a man who was destined to become the father of Australia's colonial style, the man who built the first flat-faced Georgian buildings, some with balconies, some with gazebos, all constructed from the abundant Sydney sandstone and the timber that was still plentiful. He was Francis Greenway, who had some architectural training and a death sentence for forgery. The death sentence had been commuted to fourteen years in New South Wales and, as it turned out, a place for the man in the colony's history.

These were forward-looking, hopeful times in early Australia. A sense of future was growing out of a dismal past. In 1821 a convict, Thomas McCulloch, wrote to his wife in Glasgow asking her to join him. If she came out as a free settler, he told her, she would be granted three or four hundred acres of land. What was more, she could obtain his freedom. As a landowner herself, she could have him assigned to her as labour, and together they could work the growing land. It was a fine country, he told her, and for reasons other than his liberty he would like her by his side.

There was now a pressing need for immigrants. In 1837 the Colonial Office in London approved a bounty system to encourage free men and women to break ties with home, to take the long and often dangerous voyage to the other side of the world in order to build settlements in a country about which more was being discovered every day. Under the bounty system the government paid thirty pounds to married couples, and fifteen pounds to respectable spinsters — if they were accompanied by a married couple on the voyage, presumably to keep them respectable until they reached Australia's bachelors.

Until Lachlan Macquarie's term as governor, little was known beyond the open prison which Sydney had become. Much land development had taken place to the north-west, along the Hawkesbury River, but that was less than a hundred miles away. Little had happened to the south, in the direction of Botany Bay, already rejected as land to settle on by Phillip when the First Fleet arrived. And to the west, where vast, unimagined country lay, was the stockade wall of the Blue Mountains, part of the Great Dividing Range. Here, where Sydneyites now drive to spend the weekend, it was believed an impassable barrier lay between New South Wales and something quite untouchable. The Aborigines were unhelpful; they hadn't crossed the blue-hazed hills either. A rumour spread among the convicts that China waited on the other side. Many, with dreams of a promised land, escaped only to die.

Macquarie's dreams, however, were more solidly based. When, in 1813, three brave, determined men, Blaxland, Wentworth and Lawson, did make their way across the wall, Macquarie himself soon followed and, in 1815, opened the road to Bathurst, a difficult, at times seemingly impossible route, where loads had to be virtually lifted over the mountain passes. This western route, however, finally broke the colony's mould. It opened the way that was taken by hundreds of new settlers, both free-men and emancipated; it laid before the new occupants the rest of the spreading land.

Yet, in spite of Macquarie's successes, he was not a universally popular man. Back in London, Earl Bathurst, Colonial Secretary, who was honoured by having the newly-discovered territory bear his name, was not convinced that a softer attitude toward the convicts was what was really needed to improve the morals of a felon. Less carrot, more stick, was what Bathurst wanted, and there were many in Australia willing to see that done.

40. Down among the high-rise buildings in Sydney's city centre these Victorian figures take a little sun. The oldest and largest city in Australia, with a population of over 3.5 million, Sydney is by far the most exciting in this part of the world.

41. Coxed fours row on the Torrens against Adelaide's lifting skyline. The capital of South Australia, with a population of over one million, has a growing reputation as the City of Festivals. Its Festival of the Arts takes place every second autumn in a city that is itself an amphitheatre, surrounded by the rising tiers of the Mt. Lofty Ranges.

42. *Adelaide, where a Victorian three-storied corner block is overshadowed by the high-risers behind it. A curious blend of the progressive and the sedate, Adelaide once had the reputation of being a city of 'wowsers' — sober, steadfast and demure. Yet now it boasts of establishing Australia's first legal nudist beach and of liberalising cannabis and homosexuality.*

43. *Adelaide, where these sculptures stand, began life as the capital of the only colony established (in 1836) without convict labour. For years the lack of penal taint gave the whole of South Australia a sense of superiority — because for years Australia half-hid from its past. Only recently has the country accepted how it came into being, learning to live with its history.*

44. Brisbane, another blend of old and new, of crouched stone and soaring skyscrapers. It began as a convict settlement in 1824 but in 1842 it was opened to free settlers. They flowed in, drawn by the mineral wealth and the vast agricultural potential of the colony. Today the state of Queensland has mines in the Outback, sugar and fruit along the fertile coast. Brisbane, its capital, has more than a million inhabitants.

45. Glass-walled buildings shimmer in the Brisbane River. Here, in waterside restaurants, the famous Queensland mud crab and the Moreton Bay bug, a lobster, can be enjoyed with a cool glass of excellent Australian beer. Queensland, with miles of beaches, islands, and almost sole right over the Great Barrier Reef, has seen tourism bound along in kangaroo leaps in recent years.

46. Brisbane (left) nestles among hills thick with lush vegetation. In the city itself banana trees flourish in front gardens of houses built on stilts to keep them cool. Five miles out of town is Mt. Coot-tha, where you can gaze far out to sea or inland to the Glasshouse Mts, or over the river winding in-between. Here you can take a Devonshire tea while your eyes feast on the landscape.

47. Queensland, the second largest state, was one of the last colonies to be declared self-governing. In 1859, when it came into being, like Victoria it was named after the Queen. As Queensland developed, railways were built — on a narrow-gauge track. Other colonies decided on other gauges. Such was the chaos when the country became a Commonwealth that passengers often had to change trains travelling state to state.

48. Even statues need to keep cool in Queensland's heat. As a result of so many hours of sun, Australia has one of the highest rates of skin cancer in the world. For protection, many fair-skinned noses on the continent's beaches are white or blue or yellow from thick layers of coloured creams used to keep harmful rays at bay.

49. The Brisbane River winds through the city like a sluggish eel. Its headwaters are at Mt. Mowbullan, 150 miles north, but the length of the river is double that distance due to its meanderings across the coastal plain. Here, at Kangaroo Point's Story Bridge, it carves a final bend before sauntering down to the Pacific Ocean.

50, 51. At Cairns marina, fishing boats line up waiting to take big game hunters out for marlin, or scuba divers and snorkellers away to explore the vivid life of the Great Barrier Reef. Great Barrier stretches for more that 1200 miles off Australia's north-east coast. It presents a spectacle of sea life, from shoals of brilliantly-coloured fish to giant groupers, lurking in its depths. And it is ancient: the oldest parts go back some 18 million years.

52. Cairns, Queensland's northern 'capital', lies between moody green rain forest and the blue Pacific. Gold rushes in the second half of the nineteenth century put Cairns on the map. For years tons of the yellow metal were exported through the town. Part of the old transport system still exists in the form of a narrow-gauge railway that winds up into the mountains, through tunnels of tropical giant fern. Today Cairns bustles with tourist activity, especially from May to September, in the high season.

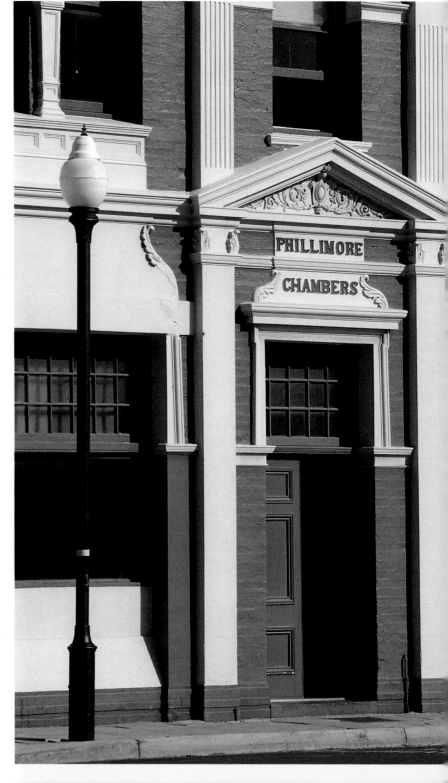

53-56. Fremantle, once Western Australia's only port, now a suburb of sprawling Perth, was first settled in 1829. Unlike many other Australian centres, it has kept most of its historic buildings, many erected by convict labour.

57-59. During the Western Australian gold rushes at the end of the nineteenth century, Fremantle became a boom town and acquired some handsome architecture like the above. For a while it faded, but today it is a busy port exporting mutton, wheat and minerals worldwide.

60. Way out on the west coast, Perth with
its million or so inhabitants is hundreds of
miles from the rest of Australia's major
cities. During the depression of 1930-33
the state felt so far removed financially
and geographically that it voted for succes-
sion from the Australian Commonwealth,
but the British Parliament declined to
receive the petition.

61. Perth, capital of Western Australia,
began as a young Englishman's dream. In
1827 Captain James Stirling sailed up the
Swan River and became convinced that the
ideal settlement could be established on its
tree-lined banks.It was not until gold was
discovered in the 1890s that Perth began to
prosper.

62. Street murals, expressions of the
Australian voice. Here in Perth a smiling
face greets passers-by. In the Sydney suburb of Redfern it might be the Aborigine
Rainbow Serpent, one of the totems of the
Dreamtime. In Coober Peddy, centre of the
opal hunters, it could show an abandoned
mine. Everywhere they flourish brightly
and are often commissioned by local
authorities to colour the urban scene.

63. Australia's reputation is as a beer-drinking nation. Australian beers are some of the tastiest in the world, even the low-alcohol variety, toward which there is a distinct trend. But the major change in the country's drinking habits has been the amazing growth in the consumption of white wine. Once treated with contempt as a sweet drink for sheilas, Aussies now accept white wine as legitimate — production has grown ten-fold.

64. Right in the north of the Northern Territory is Darwin, 'capital' of the Top End of Australia. It is a surprisingly new town — thanks to Cyclone Tracy, which ripped through old Darwin on Christmas Day 1974, destroying it almost completely. After the cyclone's Christmas present, a new Darwin was built, but the old frontier spirit is far from dead.

65. *A quiet, leafy corner among Perth's upwardly mobile office blocks. Here, as in other Australian cities, urban parks are frequent, welcome havens for office workers during the lunch hour, for old men when the winter sun is warm, for lovers any time of year.*

66. In WW I the Anzacs, Australia and New Zealand Army Corps, fought with rare gallantry, especially at Gallipoli, where thousands died, as this memorial at Port Douglas recalls.

67. In the 1930s nearly every second Australian was a member of the Church of England, about one in five Catholic. Most of the rest belonged to other Protestant churches. By the mid-1980s, however, the pattern changed. More Catholics came as immigrants from Europe, Eastern Orthodox and Asian religions began to take their place. This church in Darwin replaced one damaged by Cyclone Tracy.

68. *Much of Australia's colonial architecture was adapted from Victorian England. Curiously enough, the style was successful in its new environment. Many of the old buildings have gone now, but some remain. These formal-fronted business premises in Fremantle are reminders of the past.*

69. *Odd anachronisms occur in Australian architecture. This, the London Court in Perth, seems to belong in the heart of Tudor England. In fact, it was built in 1937. At one end of the shopping mall it has been turned into, St George and the Dragon appear above the clock every fifteen minutes. At the other end, medieval knights joust on horseback in the sun.*

70, 71. In the second half of the last century Victorian Italianate architecture became very popular. Heavy columns supported upper stories, as these Fremantle buildings show. Elaborate mouldings and cast-iron balconies adorned buildings made as proud monuments to a country that was solidly part of the British Empire.

72. However far Australia moves from England, traces of its Victorian heritage remain, as this Sydney building shows. Even if the country becomes a republic, it will retain a parliamentary system based on the British model and a judiciary with its roots in England.

73. Leaning into the city skyline, Sydney's TV tower indicates the presence of the 'box': 95 per cent of Australians watch TV regularly, 99 per cent listen to the radio. To cater for the growing immigrant population, ethnic newspapers, radio and TV stations are available in all capital cities.

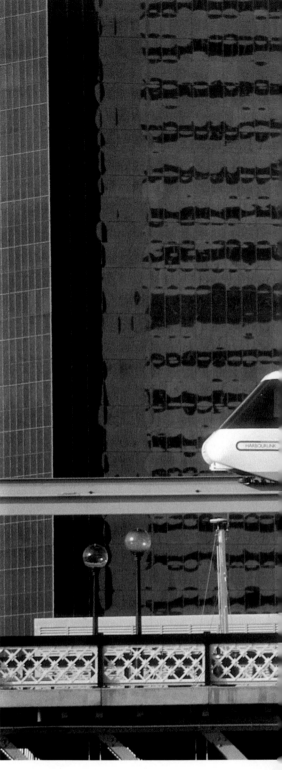

74. Adelaide's Festival Centre is South Australia's answer to the Sydney Opera House. Without Sydney's curved-shell roof line, and consequently built at a fraction of the cost, the Adelaide centre performs superbly. It contains a 2000-seat multi-purpose auditorium, an experimental theatre, a two-level drama theatre, as well as exhibition and convention halls. The many-faceted unit was completed in 1977, four years after the Sydney Opera House was opened by the Queen.

75. Sydney's monorail runs smoothly
through Australia's oldest, biggest, busiest
city, linking it to Darling Harbour, where
revitalised docklands have been turned
into a leisure centre. The monorail may
run easily at the moment but its future is in
doubt. Thousands have objected to its blue
steel track winding through Sydney's heart.
Others hate the way it flashes past their
first-floor windows. There is talk of it
being re-routed but, in the meantime, it
speeds on.

76. Beside a Roll of Honour recalling dead comrades is the scenic railway office in Kuranda, Queensland. Here, travellers in beautifully-restored old carriages arrive on the narrow-gauge railway that has brought them from Cairns, a journey that also echoes the past. The train chugs through sugar-cane fields and rolls up through rich tropical rain forests, passing the tumbling Great Baron Falls on its way to the village of Kuranda. It is a truly lovely journey through time.

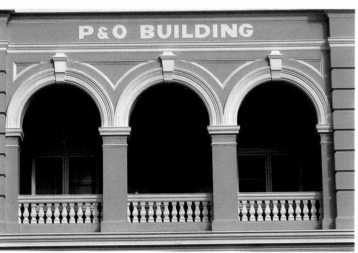

77. Wide verandahs on slender stilts, corrugated iron roofs, upper façades reflecting a Georgian heritage, cast-iron fringes adding a decorative touch, are elements typical of Australian colonial architecture. .

78. The P & O Building, Fremantle, is another reminder of an empire's past. High Romanesque arches, solid keystones, balustrades, bring back memories of men in wide-brimmed hats, brushing away the flies, pushing ever-onward in a foreign land.

The worst excesses took place on Norfolk Island, a rock over a thousand miles off the Australian coast and about three hundred north of New Zealand. Here, some of the most abominable crimes in Australian history were carried out in the name of the law, punishments so brutal that prisoners died like flies. Another hell-hole was Van Diemen's Land, as Tasmania was then called. From this part of the country the Aborigines were finally exterminated, almost as if no free-living soul could breathe its sadistic air.

In New South Wales itself, Macquarie, as governor, had more than his share of enemies. Landholders resented the increase in the number of emancipated settlers, which meant less convict labour available for allotment to their own holdings. Foremost among them was John Macarthur, another towering figure from Australia's not-so-distant past. It should be remembered that while land was being granted, convicts shipped, and the country itself explored, Napoleon's empire was at its peak, Jane Austen was writing her genteel novels, and John Nash was designing the delicate intricacy of the beautiful Brighton Pavilion. Nothing nearly as sophisticated took place on the far side of the world.

John Macarthur clashed, not only with Macquarie, but with any other in authority who crossed his path. A mastermind of the Rum Corps, he was jailed by Bligh and later sent to London to be tried for mutiny, for which he received only token punishment. He was told to keep out of public life, an admonition he almost immediately ignored. Earlier, after a pistol duel with his own colonel, he had also been returned to London to face a court-martial. From that he emerged, not only with his long nose clean — he was a handsome man with haughty features, in his portraits he appears aloof — but with the future of the Australian wool industry in his astute hands.

After the court-martial he came back to New South Wales aboard his own whaler which carried several highly-prized, pure-bred merino sheep. Not only that. Macarthur had also acquired a grant of two thousand acres of the colony's best grazing land to keep the creatures content. Once back, Macarthur began cross-breeding the English merinos with a flock he had imported from the Cape of Good Hope. The result was a hardy breed of wool-producing animals that laid down the foundations of Australia as a great sheep breeding country. It was a fortunate shot Macarthur fired on that distant colonial morning when he stood facing another in a duel. It set him on a path of personal fortune; it gave shape to the Australia of today.

And yet no matter how they towered, these great men of their day — Bligh, Macquarie, Greenway, Macarthur — there was something about Australia that defeated them in the end. Bligh was broken by the Rum Rebellion. Macquarie, in spite of the rivers, the buildings, the streets that bear his name, went unthanked for his reformations. Beaten in the end by those who resented the freedom he gave to others, he died a bitter man. Greenway died forgotten, his grave unmarked. After his patron, Macquarie, was recalled to England, Greenway's light was dimmed. Some of his buildings live on, but where his bones lie is unrecorded. And Macarthur, despite the solid building block he laid, the respect and power that surrounded him, died insane, ranting against demons, screaming at the elements he could not control.

Perhaps it all had to do with the sourness out of which the colony was born, a sourness that took generations to heal. Maybe it was the breaking of the Aborigine's Songlines, the threads that bound them to the earth. Or it might have been that the still-drifting slab of old Gondwanaland was not yet ready to submit to the violent change the white man brought to its shores. Perhaps it wanted to remain a little longer with the peace it had known through millions of years, with its kangaroos, its koala bears.

79. In 1882 Kalgoorlie didn't exist. Then, in 1883, gold was discovered. Some years later this Railway Hotel was built beside the line that brought in thousands of hopeful prospectors and took away tons of wealth dug out of the earth. Kalgoorlie's great mining days are done, but a nugget or two still turns up in unexpected places. Not so long ago a woman made a strike while installing a swimming pool.

GROWTH

The Gold Rush

The next light to shine on Australia's past was the soft, sullen glitter of gold. It was a light that altered the country's future, virtually overnight. Nobody remained untouched by its discovery, few could resist its call. It gave rise to fame and fortune, to agony, pain and bliss. It also coined the name that many Australians went by, especially during the First World War — 'digger'. A digger was simply a man who worked the diggings, the scratchings on Australia's surface, in the desperate search for gold. Later it became a commonplace, an exchange between Aussies far and wide. Like 'sport' or 'mate' or 'blue', all ways of calling a man a friend, it passed into the language, helping to make it as meaty as it is.

The Australian Gold Rush began in 1851. Edward Hargraves, an Englishman who had lived in Australia and, thanks to Macquarie's development, knew the country on the far side of the Blue Mountains, found gold in a place named Lewis Pond Creek, one hundred and seventy miles west of Sydney. Hargraves had a prospector's eye. He had been drawn to California when the rush for gold caused frenzy there and, although he didn't make a killing, he realised that the countryside around him was very similar to the hard, twisted outcroppings he'd seen back home. He returned to Sydney, set off inland to test his theory, and at the beginning of 1851, made the discovery that turned the colony upside down, inside out, blew it to the top of every news bulletin of the time.

It is fascinating to wonder what Australia's history might have been like if it hadn't been for gold. Suddenly there was no shortage of immigrants, no need for bounty-assisted passages, no hesitation about opening up the land. Within a month of Hargraves' strike, there were more than a thousand diggers scrambling along the muddy banks of the once-peaceful Lewis Pond Creek. They flowed from every other industry or profession established, or trying to establish itself, in the colony. They came with pikes and shovels, prospecting pans and sacks; they came walking, riding, pulling themselves along, with hope stamped upon their faces. Gold was for the taking; its discovery would make the humblest rich. Or so most of them believed.

And with them came those who, more often than not, were to make the real killings, to take the money from the diggers' eager hands. Behind the wave of hopeful miners were the hard-nosed men who set up bars and

Forest Creek gold diggings, Mount Alexander, Port Phillip, 1852

brothels, gambling saloons and stores. Prostitutes and con-men moved in to take what they could. There is something in the Protestant ethic, stronger then than now, that seems to condemn an easy gain as worthless. Unless a man is humbled by his work, bent by years of toil, his profit is of lower esteem, so it might just as well be tossed away as rapidly as it was garnered. In boom towns this so often happens it might as well be taken as law.

Australia was no exception. Horses were shod with golden shoes, bank notes were used to light men's pipes, a cattle trough was filled with champagne so that those who staggered across the sewer-like street could put in their heads and drink.

The country seemed rich to overflowing with nuggets, alluvial grains, sheets and pockets of lovely gold. And it didn't take a qualified geologist to realise that what seemed to cram the cracks and hollows of New South Wales would also be found in Victoria.

Victoria, a colony in its own right since 1851, the year that gold was found, had as its capital Melbourne. The city was formally established in 1837, two years after John Batman, a Tasmanian settler, rowed up the Yarra River and, in his laconic way, thought: 'Now this'd be a good place for a village.' Interesting to imagine his reaction today if he could look across the expanse of Port Phillip Bay at the glass-walled skyscrapers and the spires that fill the skyline. After all, only about one hundred and sixty years have passed since Batman saw it when there was nothing there at all.

However, no sooner was Victoria proclaimed a colony than gold fever swept through the land — with the same good and bad and ugly effects it had brought with it elsewhere. Fortune-seekers abandoned towns and settlements, rushing off to become rich overnight. At one stage there were only two policemen, out of a force of fifty, left to uphold the law in Melbourne. Of course, the town itself was pretty quiet, since most of the criminals had gone gold-rushing too. It was the same with the army. More soldiers and policemen had to be sent out from London, and probably disappeared inland just as quickly as they arrived.

The Diggers' Rebellion

As far as the miners were concerned, worse than the shoulder-to-shoulder scrambling for a find was the licence fee demanded by the government, whatever state they happened to be working in. In effect, the British Crown claimed ownership of the land — and all the riches it contained, so a licence to prospect was imposed. Fiercely opposed by the miners, at times it was impossible to collect. What is more, it banded the miners together, united them against the law — a solidarity that ended in bloody violence near the town of Ballarat, sixty-five miles north-west of Melbourne.

What triggered the outburst, it was claimed, was a bar-room brawl in the Eureka Hotel in which a digger died. The landlord, his wife and a man called Farrell were charged with murder, but were acquitted. In outrage against what they considered to be a gross injustice, friends of the dead man burned the hotel to the ground. Three diggers were arrested, and resentment against the law, against authority, against the government's licence fee, broke free.

A Ballarat Reform League was formed and issued a document demanding the abolition of licence fees, but to little effect. A month later a renewed government effort to collect licence fees caused a riot.

Diggers gathered together, built a stockade around some workings and were determined to resist the law. A State of Insurrection was declared by the authorities and the Queen's Forces were sent in. On December 3, 1854, the Eureka Stockade, as it came to be known, was attacked by a force of two hundred and seventy-six men armed with rifles, bayonets fitted. Little mercy was shown to the defiant miners. In a country which began as a prison camp, little could have been expected, but even by the standards of those harsh times, the attack was brutal.

The government forces had chosen their moment well. It was a Sunday morning, they assembled before dawn. According to a witness of the time, their attack on the Eureka Stockade caught 'men who had dined late and no doubt drunk deep'. Most were Irish, as were many throughout Australia's wild history, men who were burning to escape, to break away from or to break down a hated British system.

A list published subsequently by Peter Lalor, who signed himself 'Commander in Chief of the Eureka Stockade', cited one of the dead simply as Happy Jack. Another name to appear was that of Thonen, born in Prussia, the lemonade-man who had last been seen on the bloodied ground, his mouth choked with bullets.

In spite of the bloodshed, the diggers' resistance had a positive result. Soon afterwards the licence fee was abolished, replaced by an export fee on precious metals. Gold mining itself staggered through those first heady years to settle down as an organised industry. Once the surface metal had been scratched away, once there were no more easy pickings, the mining companies moved in. Capital was required to sink shafts, to build lifts, to operate workings underground, and by the middle 1850s the only workers left prospecting on their own were very often Chinese. They came in after the diggers, as they had done in the wake of the prospectors in California, patiently reworking the ground, resifting the trodden mud and crumbled rock, looking for a speck here, another there, to add to smaller, but much more sensibly preserved, fortunes. The Chinese put no gold horseshoes on their animals' hooves; they probably had no horses to be shod.

The presence of the Chinese at that early stage in Australia's story foreshadows the racist White Australia Policy that was to filter immigration in the twentieth century, a policy that welcomed tall, blonde, Nordic types as suitable new entrants to the land, but would have little to do with men whose skins were a different colour or whose eyes were a different shape. A music-hall song of the 1850s, called *Chinese Immigration*, jokes, only half-tongue in cheek, about how:

> *This Colony some day will be*
> *Under Chinese domination*
> *They'll upset the Australian Government*
> *This place will be their own*
> *And an Emperor with a long pigtail*
> *Will sit upon the throne.'*

Australia has always kept an eye on the great oriental powers to the north. To escaping convicts, they were places of dreams and comfort, places, as Samuel Taylor Coleridge wrote in 1816, with damsels and dulcimers, with sunny pleasure domes... Later, during World War II, they were the source of nightmares in many Australian minds as the Japanese moved relentlessly south toward the unprotected northern coastline, prepared to take over the land.

Convicts on the Run

There were others in the early 1800s who attempted to make the land their own. Almost from the moment they were landed, convicts attempted to escape. Many succeeded, for as they worked, cutting trees, grubbing the earth, they were often unshackled, sometimes unguarded. Their problem was how to survive, once away from the crude settlement. Few knew anything of the countryside; they were mostly townies, transported for robbery, forgery, theft. Not many could have survived off the land even in England, where game was plentiful, where there were gardens or fruit trees to keep them alive. In the harsh Australian climate, with only lizards or grubs to be caught, they became pitiful piles of bones, picked clean by carrion hunters more wily than themselves.

Some, defeated by the merciless island-continent, crawled back to the compounds they had run from, to be beaten, double-chained, locked in blistering holes, but at least to be given food, however vile. Others quite simply ate their companions, the weak, the stumbling, those bitten by snakes or injured by falls. Few waited for the frail to die: more often they were slain, their flesh consumed, parts of it cut off and carried away as provisions on journeys that were inevitably damned. Geoffrey Ingleton's book, *True Patriots All*, a collection of broadside, printed sheets, the newspaper articles of the time, contains page after page of confessions by men who had eaten their companions when faced with starvation themselves — hideous crimes committed by men, turned into monsters by the alien land, who had been transported for crimes no more violent than forging a money order for fifteen pounds or stealing six pairs of shoes.

Those who could not face the Outback and yet were determined to escape, set out to sea. Ships were seized, convicts took control of the craft in which they were transported, and in their efforts to avoid recapture, just as many died. Many fell prey to the, even then, notorious Port Jackson sharks, creatures that still shadow Australian shores, claiming one or two victims a year.

One notable escapee whose name passed into the history of the time was Mary Bryant, a Cornishwoman. After journeying in an open boat from Sydney to Timor, a distance of more than three thousand miles, she became known as the 'Girl from Botany Bay'. She had sailed all that distance, surviving storms, hunger and hostile natives, with her husband, two children,

The Golden Point, Ballarat, during the gold rush, 1852

and seven others eager to flee, only to be arrested in Timor when her husband, after 'words' with her, confessed to the Dutch governor who they really were. Until that moment they had passed themselves off as castaways on the north Australian shore. So much for a family quarrel!

Once more in irons, they were shipped to Java, where Mary Bryant's husband and one of her children died of fever. Finally, after being transported half way around the world again, Mary Bryant found herself in London, but alone. Her daughter had died and been buried at sea. Mary was placed in Newgate Prison, from there to be sent back to New South Wales, but by then her story was out and her courage recognised. People in high places responded. James Boswell, the biographer of Samuel Johnson, also wrote about Mary Bryant, asking for clemency and pardon. This was finally granted to the brave determined woman and the other four survivors of the gruelling journey in the open boat. Not only that, the 'Girl from Botany Bay' returned to her village in Cornwall with an annuity of ten pounds.

Bushranger Folk Heroes

Fame, or infamy, depending on your point of view, illuminated the names of other breakaways during the hard years of Australia's growth. The term 'bushranger', first recorded in 1806, was coined for Australian use. It was originally used for convicts who had broken free to range the scrubland, the forests, the unfriendly rocklands away from settled centres, but later came to apply to all rogues and outlaws, those who raised two fingers to authority. Some achieved international fame. It's possible that the best-known Australian for many years was the bushranger Ned Kelly — that is until Crocodile Dundee, and the actor who created him, Paul Hogan, came along. Ned Kelly's claim to particular fame was the metal helmet he and his brothers wore, alleged by some to have been made for them by their mother. This paints a fascinating picture of a hard-nosed Australian bushranging mum who, instead of mending her sons' socks, ran up tin hats for them to protect their heads from bullets.

Ned Kelly, together with the rest of his gang, was hanged in 1880, but before him there were others, particularly in Tasmania, which had become a convict colony in 1803. Then, forty-nine men and women, half of them convicts, established a settlement in what was called Van Diemen's Land, the name given to Tasmania by Abel Tasman in 1642, when he first sighted the island. Later, of course, the name-honours were reversed. The penal colony on Van Diemen's Land very soon became the most hated in convict lore. Second only to Norfolk Island for severity of punishment, its horrors were magnified by almost continual shortages of food or any comfort, and by a climate that was either blazing hot or mouldy to the bone.

Its reputation as bushranging country grew thanks to an inept piece of legislation by an incompetent man, Thomas Davey, Lieutenant-Governor of the colony between 1813 and 1817. He was an arrogant drunkard who loathed Governor Lachlan Macquarie, and was despised in return. He made an inauspicious, but completely in-character, beginning when he arrived at Hobart Town — he poured a bottle of wine over his wife's bonnet. Whether he was attempting to christen her arrival or expressing his dislike of what he saw has not been recorded. Shortly after establishing himself, in the hope of bringing bushranging to a halt he offered an amnesty to any who gave themselves up within six months, provided they had not committed murder. This was taken by any bushranger who could read as a *carte blanche* until the appointed date, as long as they didn't kill anyone. The crime rate soared. On the due date, few bushrangers surrendered and the free settlers became so alarmed a state of emergency was declared, martial law came into force. And the hanging began. So many bushrangers and so-called bushrangers, accused by people with grudges against them, were strung up that an island in Hobart harbour reeked with the stench of their gibbeted corpses — gibbeting was a quaint practice of hanging a man, heavily bound in chains, to show that he was a bad 'un.

Out of this hostile climate it was almost inevitable that folk-heroes should emerge. One was a Yorkshireman called Michael Howe. Although he had hardly been a gentleman-farmer back in Britain — he was transported for seven years for highway robbery — he achieved a certain Robin Hood reputation in Van Diemen's Land. No sooner had he arrived there than he escaped, formed a band of some thirty bushrangers, and declared war on what he called 'flogging magistrates' and landowners who treated their convict servants with less consideration than they gave to their animals.

For more than five years Howe kept the law at bay, hiding in the mountains and escaping across the plain. Although Tasmania is roughly circular, with a diameter of some one hundred and forty miles, government forces were unable to catch him, though some members of his gang fell into their hands. He was obviously helped by convict-servants throughout the land who knew his reputation as a fighter on their side. He must have been an oddly religious man, for all members of his bushranging clan swore their loyalty on the Bible. With a dramatic touch, he sent a letter of defiance to Lieutenant-Governor Davey written in blood. In the end, two white bounty hunters tracked him down and killed him. They took his severed head back to Hobart Town, where it was stuck on a lance and put up for public view, probably adding to his reputation.

But the Tasmanian bushranger who gained the greatest fame as a robber of the rich and a protector of the poor was undoubtedly Matthew Brady. Originally from Manchester, Brady was given seven years' transportation for stealing a grocery basket containing butter, rice and bacon. He rebelled so resentfully against his punishment, against the system, that he was given three hundred and fifty blood-letting lashes in the first four years of his confinement. They hardened his determination to resist, but they failed to break a sense of chivalry that lay deep in Brady's heart. During his trial the court-room was crowded with, what a report of the time called, 'sympathising ladies', who wept at the recital of the man's suffering. These same tender souls filled his cell with baskets of fruit, bouquets of flowers, and cakes cooked by their own fair hands.

One of the reasons for Brady's appeal to the ladies' hearts was based on an incident that involved his partner McCabe. In 1825 McCabe attempted to rape a woman whose farmhouse had been attacked by the Brady mob. Brady objected, shot McCabe through the hand, beat him up and threw him out. Left alone, McCabe floundered alone and was soon caught and hanged, but Brady's name as a protector of the fair sex was made. He also had a sense of humour that appealed to settlers. When the Lieutenant-Governor posted a notice offering a reward of up to twenty-five pounds for members of the gang, Matthew Brady put up a billboard offering twenty gallons of rum to anyone who would deliver the Governor's person to himself. However the reward for Brady was finally raised to one hundred guineas or three hundred acres of land free of all restrictions, or a free pardon and a passage to England to any prisoner who gave information leading to any one of the twelve principal characters in Brady's mob. Slowly his band was whittled away. In the end he was taken by a search party led by John Batman, the man who was one day to start the settlement in Melbourne.

Brady died on the gallows with four other men, an incident the *Hobart Town Gazette* recorded with these poignant words: 'Having mounted the scaffold with trembling step, and at the conclusion of the final prayer, which closed with the word "death" — the executioner withdrew the bolt — the platform fell, and the miserable man dropped into eternity.'

At his trial Brady faced the magistrate alongside six others, one of whom was named McKenney. McKenney and another were acquitted — a fact I personally find very fortunate, otherwise I might not be writing this today.

Land-grab and Genocide

What finally drove the bushrangers from the bush was the penning up of the land. There have been robbers and highwaymen, highjackers and waylayers down to the present day, but as settlements expanded, as more earth was turned by the plough, as coach lines and railways spread their nets through young Australia, those who attacked were more readily caught and had fewer places to hide. This expansion had a similar effect on the Aborigines; they were pushed from their homelands, herded like cattle, and put to one side.

Little effort was made by the English to understand the Aboriginal way of life, even less to get to know them as a people. They were worthless blacks drifting along the coastlines, or so the newcomers thought. They owned no land, had no buildings, wrote nothing down and spoke a variety of tongues, none of which it seems anyone made any real attempt to learn. Nor were they wanted as slave labour; the convicts were there to fill that role. Even Lachlan Macquarie, the most enlightened of Australia's early governors, failed in an attempt to introduce the Aborigines to the white man's ways. He gave a number of them a small farm near Sydney, with ground to cultivate, shanties to live in and a boat. They showed no interest in the project, preferred to sleep outside rather than in the shanties, and let the boat drift away. Then they went walkabout — to use a pidgin English expression.

Pidgin English is the lingua franca, the mixture of languages that grew out of the contact between English, Chinese and a group of Melanesian peoples, including Aborigines. The name pidgin, it seems, comes from a Chinese corruption of *business*, moving through *bidgness*, *bidgin* to *pidgin*. So that when someone said 'I come to talk pidgin' it was immediately understood that a board meeting was called for. Just as *gras bilong fes* obviously referred to someone's beard. My personal favourite is *albugerup*, a clear indication that everything's gone wrong. And *albugerup* is what happened to the Aborigines once the new settlers' greed for farmland drove them to wherever it lay available.

No Aborigine rights to the land were recognised. A New South Wales court decided in 1836 that the natives were not even free and independent tribes, with tribal homelands or areas they might call their own; they were simply drifting nomads and, as far as they were concerned, one piece of country was as good as another. All Australian territory was declared Crown Land, to be settled, granted, distributed or controlled as the governor saw fit.

As they were pushed further from their traditional hunting grounds, the Aborigines fought back. They stole rifles and used them well, they had

81, 82. Cricket arrived with the first settlers in 1788. Some early matches were contests between two players – they batted and bowled against each other while their supporters did the fielding. The first Australian team to visit England consisted of Aborigines, though this seemed to be more of a circus event than absolutely 'cricket'. The first test match between Australia and the Home Country, played in Melbourne in 1877, was a different matter. To the astonishment of the English, the men from Down Under won handsomely. (pp. 98-100)

83. Australia's most famous cricketer of all time was undoubtedly Don Bradman. Among the world's best-known sportsmen of the 1930s, he played in test after test as captain of the Australian team. Some of his batting records have never been broken. He is the only Australian to be knighted for a cricketing career. On his final appearance as a test cricketer, thousands gathered to see him play. Though Bradman never hit a ball and was out for a 'duck', this did nothing to tarnish his illustrious career.

*84, 85. Cricket teams are to be found in
every corner of the land. All aspire toward
the achievements of the Australian Test
Team, one of the finest in the world. It
plays matches against other members of
the Commonwealth of Nations, but the
highlight of the cricketing calendar is the
test matches played against England for a
trophy in the shape of a funeral urn, known
as the Ashes. When Australia beat
England, in England, in 1882 a satirical
obituary was published lamenting the
death of English cricket. At the return test
in Australia, when England triumphed, the
Ashes trophy was presented to the English
team. It has been contested ever since.*

86, 87. Although it's claimed that more
than eight million Australians are registered as taking part in various sports —
many of them would seem to be in the role
of 'active' observers. A very pleasant way
to participate. Under the shade of a wide-
brimmed hat or a sponsor's umbrella, pick-
ing up detail through field-glasses, listen-
ing to the thwack of a ball with a cool
drink at hand is one way of enjoying a
favourite sport.

88. *Australians are enthusiastic sports-watchers. The country holds a world record for a one-day attendance at a cricket match: 90,800 spectators were counted at an Australia-West Indies game in 1961, and crowds of 100,000 are claimed to watch the final of Aussie-Rules football. Here, the atmosphere seems less gripping, but the spectators are enjoying themselves. At times like this, the whole family comes along and makes a picnic of the day.*

89. *The biggest crowd-puller on the Australian sporting calendar is the Melbourne Cup. Run on the first Tuesday of November, it draws up to 180,000 people to the Flemington Race Course. The race is a two-mile classic that first took place in 1861. It has become such a day of high fashion and excitement, of bustling crowds and popping champagne corks, that it is now a national holiday in the state of Victoria where it takes place.*

90. *The game might be Scottish in origin but this course is undoubtedly Australian. Depending on the position of the kangaroos, a whole new meaning might be given to the term 'chipping in'. Golf is widely played: the climate is ideal. Most clubs are private or semi-private, but members of the public are often permitted on the course when no tournament is being held. Australian golfers, like the great tennis players of the 1950s and 60s, are today making names for themselves on international circuits.*

91. Lawn bowling used to be a game for the oldies. It was considered steady, sedate, and did not require much effort. All you had to do was put 'bias' on the bowl you rolled over the green to bring it close to the little white ball, the jack, which acted as the target. Today's competition, however, is younger, fiercer and much less sedate. Bowling has become big-time in Australia. Highly skilled teams battle for valuable prizes, individuals seek places in state or national teams. A lot can depend on the roll of a ball.

92, 93. *Most Australians live near the water and swim like fish. It has been so since the first generations of native-born Australians, known as Currency lads and lasses, were recognised as a new people growing in a distant land. In the 1820s, 30 years after the first settlers arrived, they were described as 'children of nature frolicking in the water', as swimming and diving like 'dab chicks'. This talent reached its peak in Dawn Fraser, who won gold medals in three successive Olympics.*

94. *White surf crashing, surf-boat heaving, bronzed Australians struggling with the sea. Along the continent's coastline (22,555 miles in length), surf-club members patrol the sands. They crew longboats put out to rescue swimmers in distress and compete among themselves in timing, training and skills in the surf. There are over 200 surf life-saving clubs in the country where lifeguards, men and women, give their free time day after day in the summer to watch over the safety of others.*

an understanding of the countryside which they used to their advantage, and for some ten years they hindered the white man's advance, stealing or slaughtering his cattle, burning his houses and his crops. In the years of sporadic warfare, more than two thousand homesteaders died, but in turn they killed over twenty thousand Aborigines and in the end, as almost always, the black man was defeated by the white man's tools — by his rifles and ammunition, his implements to work the land, to build houses with and to draw water, but by his spirit also, a spirit, albeit often driven by greed or lust for power, that is curiously indomitable, unyielding when there is new land to be won.

And so it was in Australia. The black man retreated, the white went on. Great rivers and vast plains covered with sun-drenched grass were discovered and opened up. The Murrumbidgee River was stumbled on by cattlemen in 1821. A giant arm of the New South Wales water system, it rises in the Australian Alps, only forty miles from the sea, but first flows north through the hills, then west across the plains before finally, some thousand miles from its source, joining the Murray River, another limb of the system — in fact, the major river in Australia, some sixteen hundred miles long. Together, they irrigate much of the finest pastoral country in the world and, with other branches of the network, drain an area as large as France and Germany combined today.

The pickings were rich for those early land-takers; they must have seen wealth and power expand around them with every step their horses took. They were not put off by troublesome natives who tried to get in their way. But if the mainland Aborigines were devastated by the newcomers, they fared better than their counterparts in Van Diemen's Land. These were, quite simply, exterminated. For forty thousand years the Tasmanian Aborigine had lived on the continent. Many believe they were the first men to arrive, to be driven south later, when other waves came down from India and Ceylon. However, it took the white man little more than seventy years to wipe them out. They were shot, poisoned, treated with sheep-dip like the animals they were believed to be.

As the country was opened up, as farmland expanded, a new type of Australian established himself in the country, taking over the tracts the Aborigine had been forced to leave. He was the squatter, who came and took with no regard for title or deed, unconcerned about possession of the land before his arrival. The squatter brought in flocks of sheep, animals that flourished on the rich grazing that spread as far as the eye could see. He put up fences, built his houses, outbuildings, smithies, batteries, stables for the horses, and gave the land an appearance it had never had before.

When the gold rush took away his shepherds, his riders, anyone in search of an easy fortune, the squatter reacted with acumen. He slaughtered his sheep, butchered his cattle and sold the mutton, the lamb chops, the beefsteaks and the roasts to the diggers with hungry bellies and the money to feed their appetites. When the surface gold was grubbed away, the squatter remained with his flocks, his buildings and his eye set clearly on the future. There were many more Australians after the gold-rush immigration. In Victoria alone, the population jumped from 77,000 in 1851, the year gold was discovered, to 540,000 ten years later, a seven-fold leap. A lot of the newcomers wanted land and resented the squatters' possessions. And so the first major wheeling and dealing, trickery and downright blackmail, entered the Australian political scene.

Laws were passed allowing a certain 'free selection' of squatted lands, provided a quarter of the land's value was paid for immediately, the rest after three years, and that the 'selector' took up residence at once. This

95. The wonders of the Great Barrier Reef can be explored by diving, snorkelling or in glass-bottomed boats. Not so long ago it was feared that it was being eaten up by Crown of Thorns starfish, which attacked the reef with their voracious appetites. Then, just as suddenly, they stopped. It appears they had turned to coral when shellfish, their natural food, was being overfished by men. The moral: if we control our appetites, they will do the same.

led to a political range-war from which the squatters emerged victorious. They set up friends or relatives, anyone they could trust, to make claims on their own land for themselves. They persuaded would-be settlers either that good land was relatively worthless or that poorly-irrigated grazings would respond wonderfully once the rains arrived. In the end, the squatters gained freehold rights to their properties, but it cost them dearly. For years they were indebted to the country's banks, and the number of political strings they had to pull gave Australia a reputation for dirty-tricks that, some would say, has persisted down to the present day. Others believe that the Australian Labor Party, the political organ of the left, grew out of the settlers' grievances and their resentment of the reins of power held by the usurpers of the land.

By the end of 1884 the law of free selection had been radically changed, but by then the shape of the country was already set in its mode. The vast landholdings remained and the Aborigine had no tribal lands in any real sense. For generations he lived in reservations away from the cities, an Outback creature in a cage, for many years not even permitted to drink unless he personally held a 'rum licence'. He could work, if he found employment, he could live among his kind, and he could come out from behind the shadow of a tree and say, 'You got some tobacco, boss?'

But if the Aborigine was reduced, other creatures survived. Sheep and cattle flourished and the rabbit became a pest. Brought to the penal colony by some of the early settlers, it ran free in what must have seemed some sort of Bunny Heaven. There were no natural predators or parasites to keep it under any control, and there was, at least in the beginning, more food than it could ever have imagined. And then, of course, the rabbit got in the way of the squatter, the settler, the small farmer — whatever name the landowner went by, his common enemy was the rabbit. Five rabbits eat the equivalent of one sheep. With grazing thinning as the herds moved further away from the irrigated plains, and the rabbits breeding in their millions, war was waged year after year with little result. Until the clever hand of man once more altered the balance by the introduction of myxomatosis.

Myxomatosis was common among rabbits of Brazil, but they had learned to survive in spite of it. Australian rabbits had no immunity. Among those that caught the disease in the first year, over ninety-nine per cent died. But that was only in the first year. In the second, the rate dropped to ninety per cent. Seven years later it was only twenty-five. Rabbits, like man, had taken to the land, had learned to survive.

Australia, by the turn of the century, had been established in its present form. The seeds of a new nation had been sown.

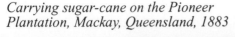

Carrying sugar-cane on the Pioneer Plantation, Mackay, Queensland, 1883

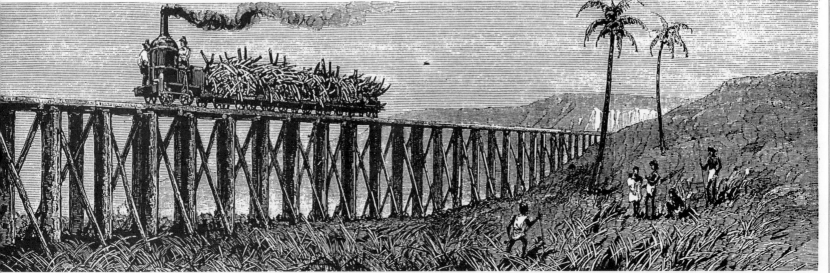

COMMONWEALTH

Toward a Nation

Australia became a Commonwealth on January 1, 1901. The last convict had been transported there in 1868. In the first eighty-one years the country had received over one hundred and sixty thousand prisoners, men and women banished to its shores. With them arrived their children, already born or about to be, conceived or delivered on the long voyage out. Australia had also welcomed many thousands more, free families who set out to work the land, to scratch for gold, to seek a future in a beckoning wilderness.

By 1861 Australia's population was well over a million, broadly divided into two main groups. There were those associated with the foundation of the colonies: the guards, marines, government officials of every description, and the convicts or ex-convicts themselves. On the other hand were landholders, squatters, merchants, and the diggers who had come for gold or any of the other minerals the country seemed to carry in a shining layer beneath its crusty surface. With them were technicians, the men with tools in their capable hands. Whether these tools were the pens and pencils that accountants or lawyers or bankers used, or the hammers, spanners, cans of oil the coachdrivers and the men who worked the railways carried, mattered little. All were put toward a common goal: the development of Australia, the building of a country that could stand upright on its own two feet.

And those to whom the new Australia mattered most, those who believed in it more and had most to gain, were the children born or reared there, who knew of no other country they could call their home. These first-born dinkum Aussies — to be dinkum in Australia is to be true — became known as the Currency lads and lasses, the children of the growing land.

Governor Lachlan Macquarie introduced the first Australian currency and granted a charter to establish the Bank of New South Wales in 1817. Until then the money in the colony had been a mixture — ducats, guineas, guilders, even rupees. Lachlan Macquarie, determined to see order in the money markets, applied to London for permission to open a bank and was refused. A man not easily dissuaded, he then imported forty thousand Spanish silver dollars and put Thomas Henshall, a convict forger, to work. Henshall cut the centre out of each Spanish dollar to make two coins, the outer, or holey-dollar as it was known, and the centre-piece or dump. They were the first Australian coins, and frowned on by the British Crown.

Even when the Bank of New South Wales issued official currency, British support was only lukewarm. Australia's new money was recognised in the colony only. In England, Sterling was the currency, and Sterling was the name adopted by those who came out to Australia, believing themselves to be English still, not really part of a new and growing nation, but a transient gentry who would one day return home, their pockets filled.

It was inevitable that rivalries should arise between the Currency lads and lasses, and the Sterling folk, and at times they were expressed in violent sport. On Friday, October 27, 1826, a prize-fight was held near Sydney between the 'Honour of old England', represented by a Sterling pugilist, George Clew, and the 'Fame of Australia's sons', Young Kable, another barefisted boxer. For twenty-five rounds they hammered each other. In the end the Sterling fighter retired hurt and the Currency lad was declared the winner, but was so badly knocked about it was feared he would die. Reporting the contest in the *Sydney Gazette*, the journalist considered the spectacle abominable. He said that it was 'neither congenial to our disposition, accordant with the principles of morality, nor honourable to them, to pride ourselves on boxing or any other European accomplishment'. He also advised that 'if certain men, who came out to this Colony, must continue with their old practices, let them horde with one another'.

He must have been one of the earliest voices raised in public protest against the behaviour of Poms — an Australian term for an Englishman. Pom or pommy, according to the famous lexicographer Eric Partridge — himself a colonial, born in New Zealand, educated in Queensland before going to Oxford — comes from Australian rhyming slang: Immigrant/Jimmygrant/Pommegrant. Whatever its origin, it is almost always derogatory. Pommy-bashing still occurs on some darkened streets.

For many years the contrary, Aussie-bashing, was a semi-official, under-the-carpet way of looking at the country's past. You can always tell a real Aussie, people joked, he's got chain-marks round his ankles. They laughed and turned away, not prepared to face the closeness of the truth. It was not until the Second World War when, once again, Australian troops proved their courage and their loyalty to the British Crown, that some sort of pride began to grow around the country's beginnings. Slowly attitudes changed. In part Australian sporting achievements saw to that. In activities that came naturally to the climate, the open spaces, the closeness to the sea, Australians can be superb. For a time world tennis was dominated by Rosewall, Hoad and Laver and the splendid Margaret Court. There are still Australians at the top. Surfing, wind-surfing and swimming have more than their proportionate share of Down Under champions. The Australian rugby and cricket teams are as good or better than any in the world.

Yet it took several generations for Australians to unshackle their convict past. Time, above all, was the great leveller. In early Australia, Currency lads and lasses began to grow strong and tall. As a group they committed fewer crimes than any other. Few of the people responsible for their being there had realised what effect a brighter, cleaner place could have on the growing mind and body. Few had considered that ample food, fresh air and the promise of hope of a new life in a new land could create upright people out of damaged moulds. The children were, literally, taller than their parents.

It was as if bodily transportation had left behind a darkness of the soul, a desperation that had no place in the new and open land. There was work to be done and new-born hands to do it. There must have been a sense of excitement in the air that had long gone stale in England. Throughout the last century Australia grew on every side.

The Pathfinders

From the beginning of the 1800s the names of the great Australian explorers became imprinted on the landscape. These were the men who travelled into vast unknowns, whose eyes gazed on seemingly unending tracts of land, rivers that flowed unhurriedly across plains as large as countries, mountains that should have been on the far side of the moon. Much of Australia, then and today, seems to have been carved by the gnarled hand of an Aborigine god.

The first of the great explorers was Matthew Flinders, an Englishman from Lincolnshire who sailed with Captain Bligh in 1791. This was not the ill-fated voyage of the *Bounty*, although its purpose was the same — to collect breadfruit trees from Tahiti. After completing his mission Bligh sailed along the Tasmanian coast and the sight of the lush, craggy landmass, still thought of as part of the Australian continent, fired Flinders' blood.

In 1795 he returned to New South Wales aboard the *Reliance* and, with fellow shipmate George Bass, a ship's surgeon, began his explorations. They sailed a small boat, the *Tom Thumb*, up and down the Sydney coast, past golden beaches, Bondi and Coogee, that would one day be covered with innumerable bodies soaking up the sun. In those distant days they were deserted, and their emptiness drove Flinders and Bass on.

Two years later, in a twenty-eight-foot whaleboat, Bass and six oarsmen discovered the strait that separates Tasmania from the mainland, the strait that bears Bass's name. They discovered the waterway but did not sail through it. That came in 1798 when Bass and Flinders, reunited, circumnavigated Tasmania. They were never to explore together again. Bass left Sydney on his way to Chile, neither he nor the ship he was aboard was seen again. Flinders returned to England determined to map more of the Australian shore. With the help of Sir Joseph Banks — President of the Royal Society, companion of James Cook on the voyage when Cook claimed Australia for the British Crown, and the man most responsible for the foundation of New South Wales — Flinders was given charge of a sloop and permission to follow his dream.

On December 6, 1801, Flinders caught sight of Australia once more and began making his maps, pressing on regardless of the fact that there were two strikes against him — his sloop was totally unfit to weather heavy seas and Britain and France were at war. In spite of this, Flinders completed the map of the Australian coastline. Between December 1801 and June 1803, dodging storms, making peace with French captains, Flinders achieved one of the most important voyages of discovery in all Australian history. But he wanted more, wanted to put more detail into the rock-lined, beach-curved shore.

His sloop, however, was a write-off, and as nothing else was available in Australia, Flinders left Sydney in 1803, bound for England, in search of a new ship. Ten days later he was a castaway on an island off the Australian coast: the ship he was sailing on had hit a reef. In command of a lifeboat, Flinders returned to Sydney and, once again, set off for England, this time as captain of the *Cumberland*, a floating gutbucket, the worst of all Flinders' unlovely craft. He was heading for Cape Town but did not make it. With the *Cumberland* leaking, the pumps failing, Flinders put into Mauritius, a French colony, and was immediately locked up as a prisoner of war.

The imprisonment ruined his health and seemed to kill his exploring spirit. When he was finally returned to London, a gaunt white-haired man of thirty-six, he was received by the Admiralty, but not well-enough; he was almost pushed aside. He spent the last four years of his life writing *A Voyage to Terra Australia*, only to die the day before the work was published. He never held it in his star-crossed hand.

If the credit for mapping Australia's shape in the waters of its many seas belongs mainly to Matthew Flinders, thanks for filling in the outline must go to several men. Sturt, Mitchell, Eyre and Leichhardt, Giles, Burke and Wills, are some of the names that ring across the landscape, names that are also inscribed in the pages of Australia's history. These are men who walked, rode horses or camels, staggered and sometimes crawled over the mountains, across the hardland, seeking Australia's heart. Strange men, some of them curiously flawed, searching for something within themselves as well as for something without.

What prompted these men to make their explorations? Can it have been, as Sir Edmund Hillary, another colonial, said about Mt. Everest — merely because it was there? Or were the men who explored Australia's interior compelled by an irresistible curiosity?

Charles Sturt, who believed that on the far side of the Blue Mountains lay an unknown inland sea, made three attempts to discover it. He found no sea, but in spite of incredible hardship, hostile Aborigines, conditions that sent him blind, Sturt navigated and mapped the southern river system, the Darling, the Murray, the Castlereigh, and enough good land to lead to the opening up of south Australia as a freeholders' settlement, not a penal colony. His courage was superb, it kept other men alive, yet he was almost a total failure when he turned his hand to anything else; he flopped in business, was unsuccessful in politics, and was not really honoured in his lifetime.

When he finally retired to England on a pension and the British government decided it was about time they offered him a knighthood in recognition of his great contribution to Australian exploration — forty years after his first expedition, twenty-four after his last — it was too late. Before the sword could be laid on his shoulder, Charles Sturt died. Like Flinders his honour escaped him.

But perhaps the most curious inland voyager of all was the ex-German student Ludwig Leichhardt, the man on whom Patrick White based his novel *Voss*. Leichhardt had no recognised qualifications as a leader of an exploring party — he was short-sighted, had little sense of direction, and had never used a gun. However, he was insatiably fascinated by the plants, the wildlife, the 'dark interior', as he called it, of Central Australia.

With money from friends, in 1844, Leichhardt mounted his first expedition with the intention of crossing the north-eastern corner of the continent, from Brisbane to Port Essington in the Northern Territory, a distance of some three thousand miles. It must have been one of the most inexperienced and youngest groups ever to leave civilisation. Leichhardt was thirty-one, the youngest member only fifteen. None seemed to know anything about living in the Outback.

For some fifteen months Leichhardt and his party struggled on, travelling much more slowly than they had planned. Men were lost in the bush, two were sent back to Brisbane, horses bolted, supplies were ruined. They discovered that by the time they had completed a quarter of the journey,

Government House, Melbourne, 1880

two-thirds of their provisions had been consumed. They were attacked by Aborigines and one man died. Food was rationed, water was scarce, their clothing rotted, they wore green-hide sandals over their worn-out shoes. Yet nothing dampened their enthusiasm, their delight in the creatures they found, their pleasure in 'sleeping under the canopy of heaven'. Nothing could break their spirit.

In December 1845, when they finally reached Port Essington, the survivors had completed one of the most remarkable and courageous journeys in the history of the Outback.

On his return to Sydney, Leichhardt was applauded for his endurance, his discovery of the rich country north of the Darling Downs. He planned a further expedition, this time to cross Australia from Brisbane, west through the heartland, and when he reached the coast to travel south to the settlement at Swan River in Western Australia.

In April 1848 Leichhardt set off into the wilderness. Neither he nor any member of his party was ever heard of again. Leichhardt's disappearance gave rise to a series of searches that lasted until 1953. Somehow or other Australia refused to accept the fact that the enthusiastic, if incompetent romantic hero had actually gone without a trace, but the mystery of what happened to Leichhardt has never been solved. He vanished into the 'kernel of the dark continent' that had captured his heart.

Once men like Leichhardt, Sturt, Flinders, and the many others had opened cracks of knowledge in the landscape, it soon began to fill. The gold rushes were one turning point, the wool industry was another. Land was taken legally, squatted-on, or grabbed, inveigled and sometimes stolen, but the lust for what it might produce drove men and women in their thousands to move in and begin their occupation.

As the country filled, the colonies, as the Australian states were known in the nineteenth century, became aware of their possibilities, their limitations and, slowly, the need for a federal whole.

A Reluctant Marriage

The idea of Australia as a Federal Nation was first raised in Britain by Earl Grey in 1848. Earl Grey, apart from being a tea-fancier, was the Colonial Secretary of the time. He felt that the colonies would need a central body to assist on increasingly important matters, as seen from Whitehall, such as tariffs, roads, railways and postal services. The idea was at first received with an indifferent Australian yawn. The colonies were power bases that none involved was eager to yield.

New South Wales, founded in 1788, was the first, and in the beginning that's all the Australia there was. But it ran from Cape York at the top of Queensland to the bottom of Tasmania, it ran inland past Alice Springs, it took up more than half the continent. As more settlements were established, more wanted the right to govern and rule. Responding to pressure, London appointed lieutenant governors to several states and, by the end of the 1850s five Australian colonies had the right to call themselves their own on local matters, although London continued to control defence and foreign policy.

New South Wales, Victoria, South Australia, Tasmania and Queensland were in existence by 1859. The Northern Territory did not become self-governing until 1978, and in the early days Western Australia remained a loner, beyond the pale, a penal colony when transportation had ceased in the other parts of the land.

Western Australia began as another visionary's fragile dream. A naval officer, James Stirling, became obsessed with the idea of founding a new colony on the banks of the Swan River where the elegant eucalyptus trees, the black swans gliding, convinced him that the seeds of England could be sown. He wanted to call it Hesperia because it faced Hesperus, the evening star. Stirling saw it as a home for free men, who would finance the colony along the lines of America's Virginia. In 1829 he and the other first settlers arrived and the colony of Western Australia was brought into hopeful being.

But the new enterprise withered under the western sun. For almost twenty years it struggled, barely self-supporting: all grain and flour had to be brought in by ship from Tasmania; most of the wool shorn from Western Australian sheep was coarse, dry, nearly worthless. Finally, in the 1800s, aid was requested from London in the form of convict labour, and with that request Western Australia set itself apart.

Anti-Transportation Leagues in other Australian states were gaining strength in their protests against shipping of felons to their shores. By mid-1851 all states except Western Australia had agreed not to employ convict labour, but the state in the west continued to rely on transportation until 1868 in order to survive. It remained outside the federal movement until the very last moment; in fact, Western Australia has stayed, in many ways, a country on its own. In the 1930s it went so far as to vote for secession, for withdrawal from the Commonwealth. Beautifully presented copies of Western Australia's case, bound in jarrah, an Australian hardwood, were taken to Whitehall, but the movement came to nothing.

The other state that showed great reluctance to joining a federal Australia was Queensland. Home to the individual, the continuing pioneer, Queensland was, and still is, largely Outback country, where cattle stations are measured in square miles rather than acres. It has its specific cultures — sugar-cane, bananas and other tropical fruits — and great mineral wealth. Gold, copper, lead, zinc, silver, iron and uranium have helped to make Queensland what it is.

I was once employed as a field geologist out of Mt. Isa in Queensland's dry north-west. Mt. Isa, I discovered, was part cowboy-town, part mining settlement. There, in subterranean honeycombs of drives and stopes, they dug out the great sheets of ore that had come up from the bowels of the planet to be laid like onion skins in the fractured rock. There, men sweated shift after arduous shift. In the mornings, evenings, afternoons, whenever they had time between the rotating twenty-four-hour work system, they drank schooners of ice-cold beer and, energies renewed, often looked for the few available women or a fight.

In the hard-baked, red-dust town there was a pub, a boozer, with white-tiled walls that were easily washed if the fighting got too bloody and the opponents could not be persuaded to settle their differences in the bull-ring out the back. The bull-ring was a square of trodden dirt where the men faced each other, swinging wild punches until one had a bloodied nose or a broken tooth, or had had enough of the shouting, the urging on, that issued from the men who watched. When it was done, and it seldom lasted long, the opponents put their arms around each other's necks, returned to the bar, and drank as much more beer as they could hold. Next day they would be underground again, concerned with each other's safety.

The first novel I published was about life in Queensland's Outback. I called it *The Hide-Away Man*, partly because it was about isolated men in that part of Australia, figures in a landscape, crawling dots between towering slabs of quartzite that glow pink and golden in the demanding sun.

98. Members of the Freshwater Club, at their north Sydney beach, manhandle their surf boat down to the sea. Australia's first Surf-Bathers' Life-saving Club was formed in 1906 at Bondi, Sydney. The new activity spread rapidly. In the 1920s there were clubs at every swimmers' beach. Their members, then all male, were the unquestioned knights of the sand.

99. *In Australia education is compulsory until 15 or 16, depending on the state. More than 70 per cent of young Aussies go to government schools, where tuition is free. There are a number of old-established private colleges, mostly run by religious denominations, based on the English public-school system. At some the English boater is still worn, together with the school tie and formal uniform.*

100-103. *Australians fought in both World Wars, in Vietnam and in Korea. Before that, as part of the British Empire, an Australian contingent went to the Boer War in 1899. Others were sent to the Sudan and China in support of the mother country. Today the Australian Defence Force, with some 70,000 permanent personnel and nearly 30,000 reserves, is kept under constant training. All over the country members of the Returned Servicemen's League march in honour of the fallen on days set aside for remembrance.*

104-106. Boy scouts or young cadets, faces lined with experience, medals catching the light, all are part of an Australian tradition, part of a loyalty to Britain and the Commonwealth, to a democracy that goes back to early colonial days. They are part of Anzac, a spirit born on the bloodied Gallipoli beaches when men fought against overwhelming odds. And although there has been no actual combat recently for Australia, that spirit of never giving in is very much alive today.

107-109. Ayers Rock, a sacred mountain to the Aborigines, a spectacular fountain of colour in changing light.

110, 111. Outback man, the lone Aussie on his horse or camped by a billabong, dog at his side, has been largely replaced by men rolling along an asphalt blacktop or bumping over dusty roads in well-sprung vehicles. And although they may still toil under the fierce sun, one eye on the weather, today's Rangers might be the sons of Greeks, Maltese or Italians. New-Australian man is now a sinewy part of the nation. Outback or urban, he represents a quarter of the population. More than four million immigrants have settled in Australia in the past few decades. And still they come, 100,000 a year and more, eager to live in the 'lucky country'.

112, 113. Stilted, arched, elegant, these colonial façades in Ravenswood, Queensland, look out on deserted streets. Once a gold rush centre, now inhabited by only a couple of hundred, Ravenswood survives, but only just.

114. More densely populated is Port Douglas, also Queensland, another former gold rush town but surviving quite successfully. Tourism has kept this fishing port alive; boats put out from here for the Barrier Reef. A cold beer helps keep the heat away — notice how many of the bottles wear coolers. (pp. 132-133)

131

115, 116. Eating out in Australia, as these signs in Cairns indicate, has moved with the changing times. Here, a German inn stands beside a health bar, down the street is a Chinese restaurant. Far fewer are the 'cafs' that served steak, eggs and chips as a regular dish. Elsewhere, Indian, Greek and Spanish restaurants are found near frozen yoghurt counters and tea rooms with herbal tea. The gastronomic face of Australia is now wide and varied. Good wines accompany meals that once might have been served with a cup of weak coffee.

117. Even an older generation of eating place, like this colonial hotel with its fili-greed façade, offer state-of-the-art services. Take-aways are to be had, even though they may be, in the main, steak sandwiches. This is, after all, a beef-raising land. Bumper stickers have been seen demanding 'This is cattle country, so eat beef, you bastards'. Australians, as is fairly well known, have little hesitation about saying exactly what they mean. And when life is fine, they're equally direct — 'No worries' covers everything.

118. Touring the country can be luxurious compared to the harshness of travel in the past. Even in the Dry Heart of the country at Ayers Rock, where noon temperatures sizzle, the comfort of an air-conditioned bus provides a travelling oasis. Tourism is one of the country's fastest-growing industries. Some two million tourists visit Australia each year to see its natural wonders, the splendid beaches, the snow resorts it offers.

119. Sydney, one of the finest harbour
cities in the world, handles much of its
local traffic, tourist traps included, with
ferries. Many residents take a ferry to the
centre of the city to shop, work or play. The
nicest way to visit Taronga Zoo, set in
native bushland with a fascinating collection of Australian animals, is by ferry. You
travel across the water, toward dark green
bush, beneath the span of the stately
Harbour Bridge.

120. Today's Australian meals may be European, Asian, Middle or South American as this Fremantle restaurant has to offer. Immigration has so greatly altered the demographic balance of the country that there are now more Maltese in Sydney than there are in Malta. Melbourne is the third largest Greek city in the world, while some 40 per cent of Queensland's Gold Coast tourist complex is Japanese owned — a far cry from the first half of the century when nearly every Aussie was of English or Irish stock.

121. The Italians with their food, clothes, zest for life, first came to Australia in the 1890s. They were among the earliest of the European immigrants. Most of them settled in Queensland, where they worked in the sugar industry. The wave of Europeans that entered after WW II contained many from the south — Italians, Greeks, Yugoslavs and Maltese. They were admitted reluctantly. Australia's first choice for immigrants had been fair-skinned types from the north.

122. Sydney Harbour Bridge was almost the longest bridge in the world at one time. Unfortunately, another, in the USA, beat it by five feet. It was built in 1932 but the cost was not paid off until 1988.

123. There is scarcely a city, town or hamlet without a memorial to those who fell in Australia's wars. The most solemn day in honour of the dead is Anzac Day, April 25. It is a national holiday in the country, as it is in New Zealand.

124. Urban murals often comment on current events. This, in Queensland, reflects in part Australia's uncertain loyalty to the Crown. For many years the Queen was accepted as Queen of Australia without question. But in 1992 it was decreed that the oath of allegiance to the country would no longer include any reference to the Crown. One day soon a referendum will be held to decide whether or not Australia is to become a republic.

141

125, 126. Sunshine, miles of scenic roadways, a warm climate, make the country ideal for cyclists of all shapes, sizes and ages. Bikes can be hired to explore with, to wander about on, or just to ride up to your favourite watering hole. In many city streets messengers on bicycles snake in and out of busy traffic, helmeted for safety. If an Aussie tells you to 'get on your bike', you've outstayed your welcome, it's time to go.

127. Sydney's Darling Harbour used to be
acres of abandoned docks, railway yards,
warehouses used in the early part of the
century for wool, hides, products from the
land. In 1984 the New South Wales government began a revitalisation programme
that has resulted in a huge tourist and
leisure park with museums, shopping malls
and gardens set on the water's edge. It is
linked to the city centre by a monorail that
runs through Sydney's narrow streets at
first-floor level, zooming over the heads of
pedestrians below.

128. Australians, some say, will bet on anything, even two flies crawling up a wall. They have the reputation of being the heaviest gamblers in the world. On Melbourne Cup Day, first Tuesday each November, millions of dollars are wagered on a single race. The Sydney Opera House was financed through a lottery. There is no shortage of places to have a bet. There are state-run lotteries, off-course betting through totalisator agencies, poker machines and casinos. Here, in Alice Springs, a punter sorts out the odds on a camel race.

129. The Camel Cup in Alice Springs is raced for every May. Camels were introduced to Australia in the early days to carry ore from mine workings to the mill, their 'desert' qualifications making them perfect for the task. Over the years many escaped or were released into the countryside. There may be as many as 30,000 wandering the northern states today. Some are left in peace. Some can be hired by tourists to ride through a desert sunset to a wine-tasting. Others gallop for the money in Alice Springs.

130, 131. Australian waters have an unsavoury reputation as far as sharks are concerned, but the chances of being attacked are something like one in a million if you swim off patrolled beaches where helicopters scan the waters and shark nets are in place. Most shark attacks have taken place in less than six feet of water, late in the day, no more than fifty feet from the shore. Shark-fascination is catered for by aquariums such as this in Cairns. The creatures are fished for sport from resorts like Port Douglas, above.

132, 133. Captain Cook looks as if he might have wanted to prevent it, but nothing stops the earth being torn apart when there are diamonds to be won. The Argyle open-cut diamond mine in Western Australia (overleaf) is on one of several new diamond fields discovered in Australia in recent years. The white, amber and rare pink gems found here have helped make Western Australia the wealthiest mineral state in the whole country and have put Australia itself close to being the world's biggest producer of industrial stones.

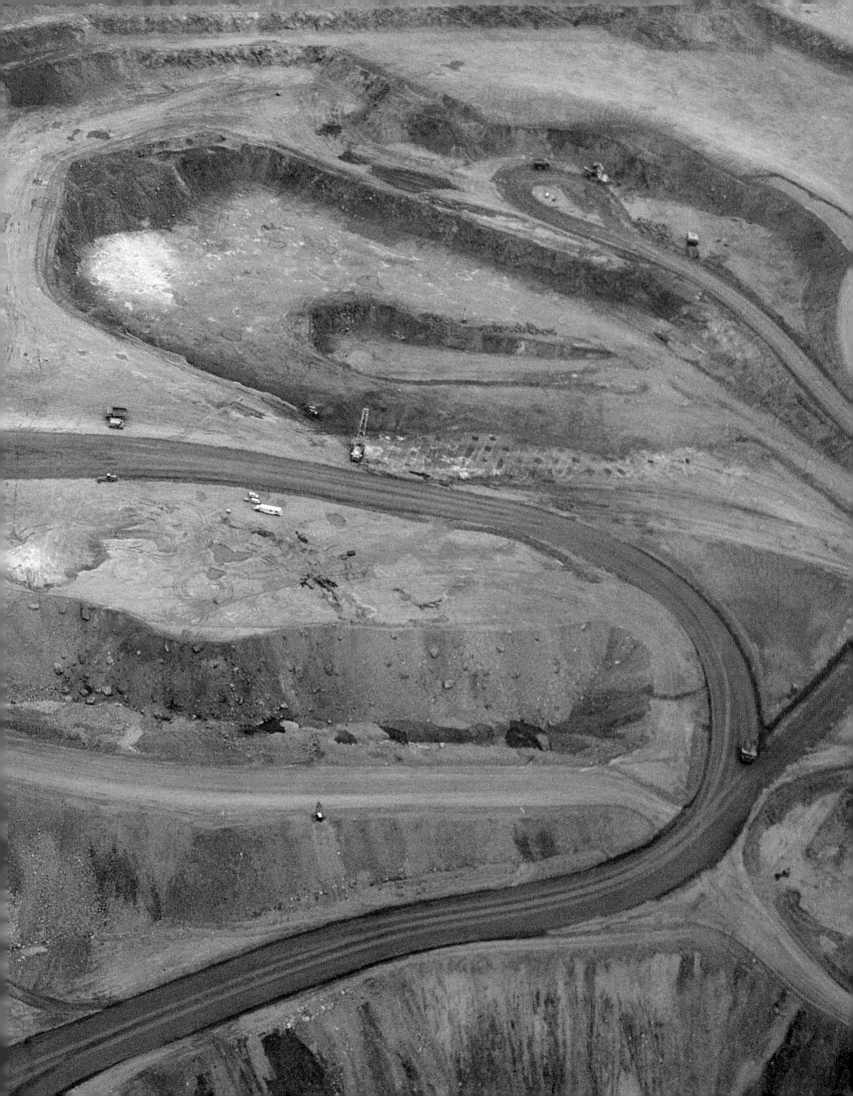

134, 136. Not only diamonds are taken from Australian earth. Gold and silver, lead, copper, iron, nickel, manganese, uranium and zinc lie in seemingly endless layers beneath the country's surface. Each time a new discovery is made, Australia moves closer to the top of the mineral-producing list. Coal, oil and natural gas also come out of the land. Bauxite, some 43 per cent of the world production, is carved out of Australian mines, like this in Weipa, Queensland, where giant machines rip open the earth.

135. Other Australian machines perform gentler functions. This vehicle, at Kakadu National Park, Northern Territory, is used to patrol, to preserve and to guide tourists through the vast tropical parkland in one of the most untouched areas of the country. Kakadu protects an entire major river catchment system — the South Alligator River and all its feeding creeks and tributaries rising in the Arnhem Land plateau. This 'mini-state' with its irreplaceable variety of plant and wild life is so important that much of it is on the World Heritage list.

They were men who had learned to survive, as had the animals they shared the landscape with. Once I saw a camel lumbering across the skyline. When I mentioned it to a gnarled man in a dusty pub, he told me they had been common once, brought in to carry ore. 'Them and the goats,' he added. 'Often see them together.' When I asked about the goats, he laughed and told me that the wood-frame ore packs often cut through the camel's hide, so a goat would be killed and its skin sewn over the hole in the camel's back. He grinned and rubbed his bristled chin. 'One of the first skin grafts ever, I'd reckon,' he added. 'Like another charge?' — his way of suggesting a beer.

I wrote about men who drove battered vehicles through the heat and clouds of grinding dust, scavenged old mine workings, scraping a living from forgotten ore-loads, where roof-support timbers were rotten, where there was practically no safety at all. Men who spent their lives fencing properties, mile after mile digging holes, placing peel-bark gum posts in the unwelcoming earth, linking each post with three strands of barbed wire. The fencers were as stringy and tough as the posts they planted; they could be as prickly as the wire they strung.

And with the men in the parched and brittle Outback were the creatures who kept them company: galahs, pink and grey cockatoos, squawking in huge clouds of colour and vitality. At times, when there was no water elsewhere, galahs gathered on the rims of corrugated-iron storage tanks. While the water level remained high the birds dipped their beaks and drank. As it sank they remained, claws scraping the iron, hanging on in hope until they fell, flapped weakly for a moment or two, then floated dead, pink and grey bundles of feathers.

Then there were the brolgas, the native companions, the dancing cranes, with their mating ceremony of delicate steps, patterns more intricate than an Aborigine corroboree. They danced in soft, milky morning light, their choreography stylised, making delicate swooping steps toward each other, lifting the red dust with their wing tips.

I was looking for copper in the brittle land, but found none. Instead I was shown an aspect of living I have seen nowhere else in the world. They were hard, the men and animals that shared the landscape. Some failed, some survived superbly, some followed a fine line that ran between madness and sobriety. But in every respect they were vitally alive and, for the time I was among them, I was grateful to be able to share their spirit, their primitive joy.

The Final Bonding

When a basis for an Australian Commonwealth was finally accepted, in 1900, by all the states involved, one of the conditions was to be the establishment of an Australian Capital Territory, a new state on its own, with a new city built as its centre at least one hundred miles away from Sydney, to cut the roots of the old colonial power. This, the states agreed on. They agreed also that Australia was one nation, white and Christian; they were afraid of immigration from the north, those who might come who were not a similar people, who might edge them from their land.

Toward the end of the last century foreign colonisation had been active all around them. Russia was probing for places in the North Pacific. New Caledonia and the New Hebrides had been annexed by France. Germany had moved into Samoa, part of New Guinea and had taken Nauru. Australia feared part of its coastline could be next.

So the states moved together as one on this. But in other areas they remained untouchably apart. When railways were crawling their way across the great Australian landscape, there were several states that refused to conform to a standard gauge. There were, and still are, three different widths of track in the country. Until 1962, if you wanted to travel by train from Sydney to Melbourne you had to change trains at the border. Sleepy passengers — it usually took place at 2 am — and freight had to be shunted from one set of wagons to another.

However, on January 1, 1901, Australia became a Commonwealth, some twenty-five years after the first legislative steps were hesitantly taken. At the beginning of the twentieth century Australia's equivalent of the Maastricht Treaty was turned into a working reality. Australia, the collection of colonies that had fielded a national cricket team against England since 1862, finally became united in more than defending three upright wickets against a hostile ball.

But thirteen years more were to pass before Canberra, the federal capital, was founded. The first stone was laid in 1913 in what began as a curiously un-Australian development. It was as if, by separating a federal territory, the other states were prepared to put its urban design and content into a stranger's hands. Like the Sydney Opera House, some forty years later, a design for Canberra was made the subject of an international competition. It was won by Walter Burley Griffin, an architect from Chicago.

The site chosen for Canberra was a hundred and fifty-five miles south-west of Sydney, near the foothills of the Australian Alps, a lovely setting that somebody cynically described at the time as a great sheep paddock about to be ruined. But not without a struggle. Walter Burley Griffin, who had worked with one of the most visionary architects of modern times, Frank Lloyd Wright, was to find that his plans became so radically altered by Australian boards, bodies and committees that he set sail from the United States to try and salvage his original ideas. This also was repeated forty years later when the Danish architect's design for the Sydney Opera House was modified by men in government. Then Jorn Utzon, the architect, took a trip in the other direction; he left Australia and went back home.

After his arrival in Canberra, Griffin battled for six years, attempting to restore his original design. He barely succeeded in retaining the basic idea. His vision of a new-style city in a newly formed land was whittled away by the sharp pencils of bureaucracy. Hard-nosed, pragmatic Australian politicians had little time for the American they described as a Jack of all trades, a man they suspected of being an artist, not a practical fellow.

Today Canberra looks a little more like the city Griffin planned. His original idea of ringed streets, growing as they circled out from the centre, like a cobweb spread on the land, has been largely achieved. The formal gardens and the lakes have been created. Lake Burley Griffin, one such, named after the man no one welcomed at the time, was finally constructed in 1963. The man himself remained in Canberra for many years after he was pushed aside — designing public incinerators, some of which are considered to be among the finest examples of his work.

In 1927 the Australian Federal Parliament moved to Canberra from Melbourne. Over the years the National Gallery was established there, as were foreign embassies, a university, the Australian Academy of Sciences and the National Library. Canberra is the functional heart of Australia, but it is not the country's soul. For all its wide, handsome streets, its neo-classical buildings, it lacks the feeling of a city, a place where people have lived and toiled, have died and struggled to be born. Designed to function, it did not grow out of human pain and joy.

But with Canberra Australia put the stamp of legitimacy on its right to stand as a nation. It adopted its own national flag — the stars of the Southern Cross, a design quite like the banner flown by the defiant gold diggers when they defended the Eureka Stockade, with the British flag placed in an upper quarter. The country has its own coat of arms, also similar to the British, but instead of a lion and a unicorn, on either side of the shield there is an emu and a kangaroo.

Like an ungainly child, Australia was ready to go forward into the twentieth century, looking for security, seeking acceptance in an adult world. Restless, at times blinkered by its history, it hid for a while from its convict past, closed its doors to others who wanted to come in from the cold. But, steadily in the warm southern sun, like the Currency lads and lasses, the country grew tall and upright, at times defiantly proud, with a clear sense of its own identity.

And from its unruly beginnings, from its place of fragile imbalance between old Europe and the Asian north, Australia has produced a people with its own voice in the world. That voice has become increasingly mixed as immigration boomed after the Second World War — some four million emigrants have arrived since then — but more settled in its tone. Australians are proud of what they are: direct, sometimes blisteringly forthright, and until very recently devotedly loyal to the British Crown.

They are also a creative people. The country has produced a line of talent disproportionate to its population. Great actors, writers, film-makers, painters and dancers have sprung from the country's relatively immature loins, men and women who, by sharing their creative capabilities, have received world-wide applause, and made a notable contribution to the arts on the international scene.

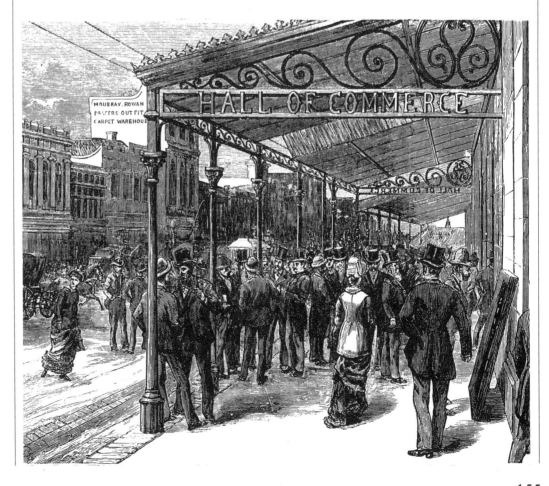

Melbourne Stock Exchange, 1880

THE AUSTRALIAN VOICE

The Native Tongue

The Australian voice, as an instrument, has not always been applauded. In 1911 an American, William Churchill, commented that 'Australian English represents the most brutal maltreatment which has ever been inflicted on the mother tongue'. Many Britons, who take a similar view of American English, would agree. As recently as 1972, Lord Casey, governor general at the time and himself Australian-born, remarked that he could not believe 'that English is tortured anywhere else in the world to the same extent as it is here'.

As early as 1820, Australian English was recognised as something apart, an amalgamation of dialects from all over the United Kingdom with a special Irish touch. Aboriginal words were part of the vocabulary: boomerang, billabong and kangaroo were commonly used, and descriptive phrases, newly-minted words and expressions describing the vigorous life in the extensive land, were added to the tongue as time went by.

Before long, countrymen were referring to places that lay 'beyond the black stump', meaning in the Outback, in the distance. The black stump referred to was one of many that dotted the hillsides, left behind when the need for timber for housing, fencing, mines, led to wholesale destruction of forests. The same countryman might have easily said 'out in the woop-woop' to indicate a similar remoteness. Woop-woop was a way of satirising Aboriginal place names that were often double-barrelled, such as Wagga Wagga.

And the song that almost became the Australian national anthem, *Waltzing Matilda*, has lines practically unintelligible to anyone not familiar with the local voice. *Waltzing Matilda*, a term that on its own means 'going walkabout', taking to the bush, was written in 1895 by A.B. 'Banjo' Paterson, a Sydney journalist turned bush balladeer. He called himself Banjo after a racehorse he fancied. In a national poll conducted throughout Australia in 1977, the rather more doleful, but certainly more respectable, *Advance Australia Fair* was voted national anthem, *Waltzing Matilda* came second. *God Save the Queen*, or *King*, which had been the country's anthem since 1788, when the First Fleet arrived, came third, although it was agreed that it would be played in public when any member of the royal family was officially present.

But *Waltzing Matilda* is close to the Australian heart. It echoes a freedom and an independence that belongs to the vast open country, to roots that go back into the penal past. At the end of this lengthy ballad, like all good folk heroes, the swagman protagonist dies. 'You'll never take me alive' are the last words he defiantly cries. Then he jumps into the *billabong*, the cut-off end of a meandering river bend, under the shade of a *coolabah*, a eucalypt, a type of box gum tree. Behind him this swagman, a tramp with a bag over his shoulder, leaves his *billy* boiling on a camp fire — a billy is a can with a lid, like a kettle without a spout or handle, used to carry and boil water for cooking or making tea. The name is said to have come from *billa*, the Aboriginal word for water. And what the song is all about is the swagman's confrontation with a *squatter*, a landholder, over a stolen *jumbuck* or sheep. The name jumbuck seems to have been derived from the Aboriginal word for a white mist, the closest the Australian natives could come to defining a flock of sheep, as new to their bewildered eyes as was the sight of a man with white skin wearing multi-coloured garments.

So it is easy to see why the Aussies nearly voted for *Waltzing Matilda* as the anthem to represent the country. It has many of the ingredients of a growing, proud, defiant nation, including a vocabulary that sets them apart.

As does the language as a whole. There are at least twelve words or phrases for vomit, ranging from the gentler 'technicolour yawn' to my personal favourite 'shouting Europe at the sink' which has a fine onomatopoeic ring to it. The range for such a basic function is not surprising. Australians rank third in the world as beer drinkers, staggering in behind the Germans and the Czechs. They may even be second now that Czechoslovakia has broken up.

Perhaps the finest analysis of the Australian language was made by Alistair Morrison in his *Let Stalk Strine* (Let's Talk Australian), a book which began as a series of newspaper columns in the *Sydney Morning Herald*. This delightful, if slightly exaggerated, presentation of Australian, or Strine, is said to have been based on an experience Monica Dickens, the English writer, had while autographing books in an Australian shop. As she busily scribbled 'To Sally or Alice or Joe with best wishes', a voice in her ear said 'Emma Chizzet'. So Monica Dickens reached for another copy and began: *To Emma* when the voice interrupted. 'No, emma chizzet? Wots it cost?'

From this came Strine, in which equipment to control the temperature in a room is known as an *egg nishner*. And something to eat between two pieces of bread is a *semmich*. I personally like the title of the old love song *Tiger perra sparkly guys* (Take a Pair of Sparkling Eyes).

However, on a more elegant level, some amazing prose has come from the pens of writers like Patrick White, winner of the Nobel Prize for Literature in 1973. White, although born in England, went to Australia when he was six months old to be brought up on his father's sheep farm. Educated in both Australia and England, White developed a critical eye, a prose style that was both precise and sweeping, and a view of his country that was all-encompassing. It embraced the Sydney typist who, in a moment of embarrassment, seems to have 'too many prawn shells sticking to her fingers', and pioneers, explorers, men like Stan Parker in *The Tree of Man* or the eponymous hero of *Voss*, who were driven by the land, possessed by daemons of purpose. Patrick White saw into the Australian heart; at times he seemed to hold it in his hand.

Australia saw a flowering of writing, and painting, at the end of the nineteenth century, when Federalism was being accepted, when national feeling was high. Then men like Banjo Paterson and Henry Lawson, sometimes credited with being Australia's greatest short-story writer, gave shape to the myth of the bushman, those who worked and walked the land. Another lifting of the Australian voice occurred in the 1960s. It also coincided with a time of re-focussed nationalism, and the two are undoubtedly interlinked. At the beginning of the 1960s Britain, the Mother Country, the place many Australians still thought of as Home, began negotiations to join the European Economic Community, a step that would inevitably mean loosening ties with Australia and other countries that were part of the Commonwealth.

Many Australians felt betrayed. They no longer had a ready market for butter, wool or meat. Men who had responded immediately to a call to arms in two world wars when Britain needed them felt as if they had been used and tossed aside. Out of this resentment grew a harder, more realistic, sense of what Australia was and, more importantly, what Australia could be. While the men who controlled the export markets looked for new customers in the north and to the east, while they courted Muslim clients for mutton, Japanese manufacturers for their wool, Australian writers and painters, musicians and choreographers were directing their talents inward, looking deeper into the country's soul.

Other important nationalist effects began to make their mark about this time also. For the first time in the country's history, in 1962 the Aboriginal people were given the right to vote. Considered subjects of the British Crown, and later of the Commonwealth, for far too long they had been virtually non-persons, pushed aside and left to decay. Now they, too, were being given their voice. And, at the beginning of the 1960s, oil was proved to exist in commercial quantities in Queensland. The nation, as a whole, was on the edge of stepping forward, cutting the umbilical cord that, since its first ugly, squalling days, had bound it to Mother England. As if to confirm this, immigrants were pouring in from other parts of Europe, many on assisted passages. A new wave of 'bounty' citizens, of a magnitude not seen since the 1850s when the gold rushes began, started a population boom that saw a virtual doubling of Australia's numbers.

Those who came were not all British. Many were from Italy, Greece, Germany and the Netherlands, others from the Asian north. New Australians they were called, a term that passed into the language. As I was being driven home, late one night, by a Sydney taxi driver, a drunk staggered across the road oblivious to the traffic. 'There's one of them temporary Australians,' the driver muttered as he swerved around the man, moving the term a little further ahead.

As the newcomers came and filled the land, they brought with them attitudes, religious beliefs and customs that were to change Australia forever. Greeks and Italians opened corner stores, took over groceries in the towns, moved into city 'delicatessens', where they introduced a range of sausages and cheese, of pickled vegetables, herbs and oils that the Australian palate at first resisted, but quickly grew to love.

The newcomers came but they did not conquer; they moved in but they did not eject the old. They modified, they polished, they added delicate touches to the diet, but the 'jolly swagman' image of the Outback man, Banjo Paterson's *Man From Snowy River*, or Patrick White's pioneer did not die. He surfaced again quite recently in the shape of Crocodile Dundee, a little smoother, slightly more sophisticated, but still recognisable as the man prepared to take on anything, the man who would have a go — even in New York. *Voss* has been turned into a ballet by the choreographer Richard Meale with the libretto written by David Malouf, grandson of an earlier wave of New Australians that arrived in the 1880s.

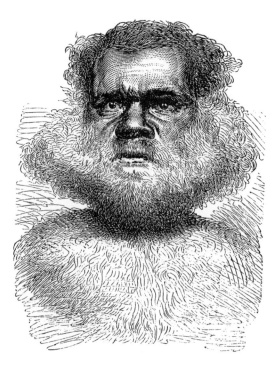

Aborigine man of New South Wales, 1857

A New Dreamtime

The stimulus of separation from the old English ties, the new faces in the Australian crowds, the industrial activity, the size of the crowds themselves, lifted the Australian voice to new heights. Broadcasting announcers, those who did the voice-over for commercials, actors on stage, in the expanding film industry, gradually stopped trying to polish their accents, to carefully pronounce their Ts and Rs or feeling a little self-conscious shouting 'Car Park' across a crowded international room — a long high A being a dead give-away.

Amongst those who had most to gain, and who are still gaining, were the Aborigines, the original owners of the land. They had been pushed aside when the white man came, literally transported away from the growing urban centres around the Civilised Rim to distant reservations, places where they were out of sight of the rest of Australia, and very much out of mind. Until the Second World War, when many of them proved their bravery, most pure-blooded Aborigines could be made to live on a reservation in the hot, hard Outback, where they were supervised by government officials, missionaries, nurses or teachers who were stationed there, and taught to get on with their lives as best they could.

This was an anachronism, out of time with Australia's new-found honesty, designed to be remedied as the country forged ahead. Besides, with the 1960s came the increasing importance of the media, the public screen where errors, injustices, sins both large and small, could be brought before the people. And one of the injustices brought to trial beneath harsh lights and probing cameras was the marginalisation of the Aboriginal people. The desperation of many of their lives, the waste of their talents, their knowledge and their skills, was appalling. They had survived on the dry and drifting continent for some forty thousand years before the white man arrived. No one will ever know what has been lost by reducing their tribal knowledge, by forcing them to adopt a lower position in society than the transported convicts who helped push them aside.

Perhaps the sad circumstances surrounding the jail sentence received by the Aborigine painter Albert Namatjira in 1958 first drew public attention to the double legal standard under which the Aborigines were made to live. Namatjira, like just about every other Aborigine, was brought up on a mission station in a tribal community that was instructed in the Christian faith. From his birth he was a man hung between two worlds; in the end he died between them.

The mission, being Lutheran, was itself policed during the war because of possible German connections. When free to operate, it made souvenirs, bits of painted bark, carved woods, to sell to tourists in order to survive. Namatjira showed talent. One of the officers on duty during the war was Rex Batterbee, a Melbourne water-colour artist. Batterbee encouraged Namatjira, gave him lessons, presented some of his paintings in an Adelaide exhibition and later became his agent. And so the Aborigine painter, the artist from the reservation, was launched. The truth is that the public, certainly at first, was more interested in the man than what he produced. His paintings were considered derivative, white man's work not native art, but the fact that the blackfellow could manage brush and palette at all was something to take notice of.

In those days most white Australians never saw an Aborigine. What they knew of them was based on photographs of bubble-nosed, heavy-browed, bearded men sitting half-naked with a spear on a sunny rock. Males were referred to as Jackie, regardless of their name, in the same way that black Americans were called 'boy' in the South. Aborigine women were Marys, if they weren't just called 'gins'. No full-blooded Aborigine was allowed in town after dark; he had to be safely back on the reservation, as Albert Namatjira found to his distress when, as a successful painter, he tried to buy a house in Alice Springs. Nor were Aborigines allowed to drink. White man's liquor was not for them. Some, under certain circumstances, were given a rum licence, or a grog licence as it was more commonly known, but the rest were legally teetotallers whether they liked it or not.

This, in the end, destroyed Namatjira. As one of the first full-bloodied Aborigines to be granted, in 1957, full Australian citizenship, he had the right to call most of his life his own. Though still unable to vote, a right that was not extended to Aborigines until 1962, he was more or less a free man. He had been awarded the Coronation Medal and he had been presented to the Queen when she visited the country in 1954. But he was still a man strung out between two worlds.

He was a bread-winner, a provider for his tribal relatives, and the more famous he became, the more relatives appeared. There was a time

Aborigine woman of New South Wales, 1857

138. To the geologist they are fossilised trees, to the Aborigines part of the Dreamtime when heaven and earth were one, when plants and animals, men and women were all of a single spirit. Then the white settlers came and the Aborigines' culture was dismembered. Only today are science and ancient belief living together in some harmony. That the Pinnacles at Nambung, Western Australia, remain steadfast in the desert must give heart to many an Aborigine.

139. Off the Queensland coast lies Lizard Island, the most northern of the islands of the Barrier Reef. Lizard looks today as it must have done to less kindly Aborigines who chased Mary Watson, a settler's wife, to sea in an iron pot, legend has it. Anyway, she fled with her son and a Chinese cook, and all three perished a few days later. (pp. 162-163)

140. Like the great serpent the Aborigines believed formed the undulating shape of the nascent earth, the Carpentaria River meanders over its flood-plain in Queensland. (pp. 164-165)

141. The brooding coast of Tasmania where the Aborigine people suffered most at the hands of white settlers. Deprived of their fishing grounds, forced from their hunting territory, shot, abducted, their women taken, the Tasmanian Aborigines were reduced to a few dozen only sixty years after the English came. These were then herded into camps, where they too died — the worst case of ethnic cleansing in British colonial history. (pp. 166-167)

when he was supporting more than five hundred of them a week. This did not seem to worry him, but the fact that he couldn't share a drink with them did. The inevitable occurred. In August 1958 Namatjira was charged with supplying liquor to Aborigines and sentenced to six months hard labour. He appealed but the appeal was dismissed, just as his two other appeals to live among the white man had been denied — before he was given a piece of paper telling him he was an Australian with the right to live in his land.

Following a public outcry, Namatjira's sentence was reduced. He served two months, but the conflicting demands of the two worlds in which he tried to exist finally destroyed him. He died of a heart attack less than three months after being released.

Namatjira's death focussed attention on the plight of his people. The 1960s saw the first step towards righting the social injustice the Original Australians had been subjected to for so long. Though the movement began slowly, there has been steady progress. In 1960 the social security system was amended to allow Aborigines greater access. In 1965 a new leader emerged, Charles Nelson Perkins, the first Aborigine to graduate from the University of Sydney. He led what he called freedom rides through New South Wales, protesting against the conditions many Aborigine workers had to endure, the token wages they were paid — quite often they were given flour, tea, sugar, salt beef and tobacco. When they were given money, it was less than a white man earned. In 1966 a Commonwealth Arbitration Commission decided that all workers should be paid the same whatever the colour of their skin.

More was to follow. A landmark referendum in 1967, held to decide if white Australians wanted Aborigines to be included in the national census, approved this by a majority of ten to one. Until then Section 127 of the Australian Constitution had decreed that 'Aboriginal natives shall not be counted' when 'reckoning the numbers of the people of the Commonwealth'. Until 1967 they did not belong to the so-called civilised group. Once recognised, however, once their voice was heard, Aborigines began to demand the return of their land, especially places they considered sacred.

In 1968 the first important land-rights test case came before the Australian courts. A number of Aborigine tribes contested the granting of mineral leases to a mining company in the Northern Territory. Publicity was intense. John Gorton, Prime Minister at the time, stated categorically that the Aboriginal demands for the return of the land would not be met. This was confirmed by the courts. It was ruled that the Aborigines had no rights to the land they had lived on for generations. The issue became a major one in the elections that followed in 1972.

Gorton's government lost the election. The in-coming Prime Minister, Edward Gough Whitlam, appointed a High Court judge to look into the matter. The recommendation that Aborigines living on reservations be given freehold title to the land finally passed into law. By 1983 twenty-eight per cent of the land in the Northern Territory had been given back to those who lived on it. Perhaps the most significant return of property from the Aborigines' point of view occurred in 1985 when Ayers Rock, that massive bump of red sandstone lifting over eleven hundred feet into the air in the Northern Territory, was given back to the Pitjantjatjara people.

Ayers Rock, one of Australia's tourist attractions, its display of changing, moody reds at sunrise and sunset known all over the world, is called Uluru by the Aborigines to whom it belongs. Uluru is where one of the Aboriginal ancestral beings, the rainbow serpent, the carpet snake, whose slow, sliding movements across the land pushed up mountains and

142. The Aborigines were a nomadic people, sleeping beneath bark shelters, hunting game, fishing with pronged spears bound with sinews from the kangaroo. Their knowledge of the land enabled them to find water where none appeared to be.

143. Aborigines began arriving in Australia during the last Ice Age. They came in several waves from India or beyond, making the final step to the Australian land mass in canoes or on bamboo rafts. When the ice melted and the seas rose again, the Aborigines and the animals they shared the continent with were cut off from the rest of the world.

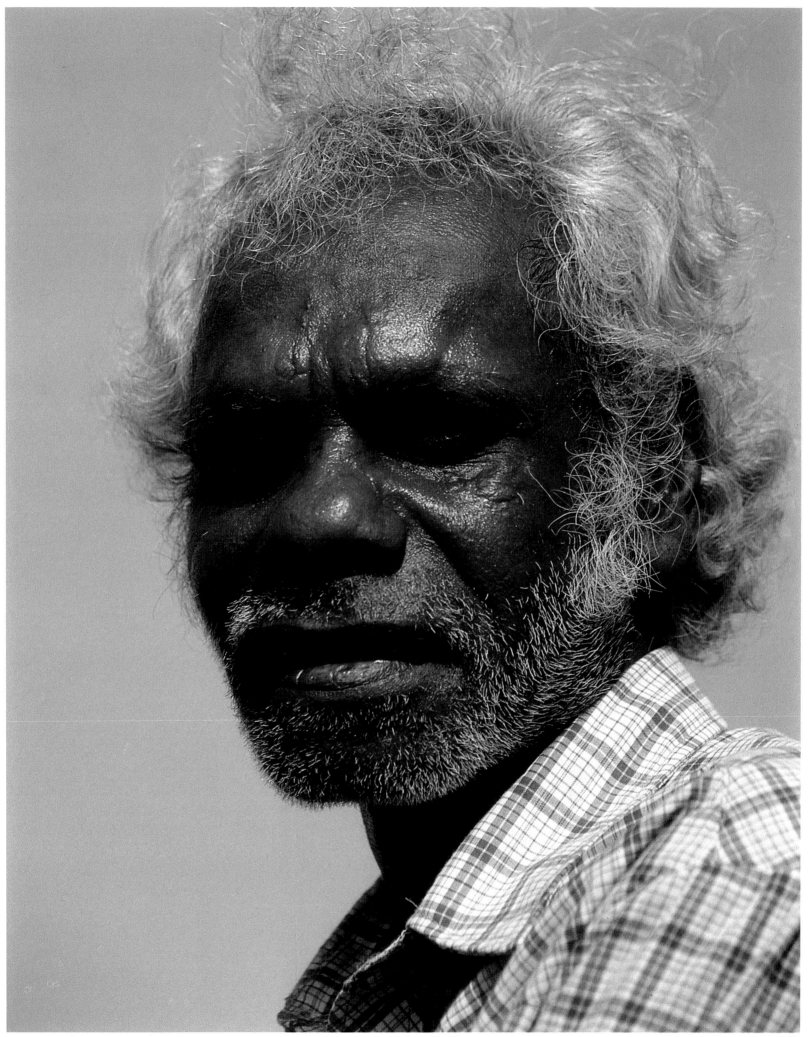

LIQUOR ACT
WARNING
RESTRICTED AREA

THE POSSESSION OR CONSUMPTION OF LIQUOR
IN THIS COMMUNITY WITHOUT A PERMIT IS A SERIOUS
OFFENCE.
• VESSELS CARRYING LIQUOR MAY BE SEIZED AND FORFEITED
AND THE FOLLOWING PENALTIES MAY ALSO APPLY.

FIRST OFFENCE: UP TO $1,000 FINE
                  OR 6 MONTHS GAOL

SECOND OR   UP TO $2,000 FINE
SUBSEQUENT   OR 12 MONTHS GAOL
OFFENCE:

144-147. *After the white settlers took over the land, the Aborigines were captive in their country, bottom of the social ladder, placed beneath the convicts transported to their shores. When they resisted, they were slaughtered, hounded into the reservations, deprived of their ancestral grounds. They could not vote, drink alcohol, or spend a night in any town. Australia tried to forget them. Only very slowly have their rights and their significance been recognised. Soon there will be some 300,000 Aborigines, the same number as were in the country when the white man came.*

WARNING

Estuarine crocodiles inhabit most
rivers swamps and lagoons
throughout Cape York Peninsula

148-151. Crocodile warning signs in crocodile country, Kakadu National Park in the Northern Territory. There are two types of crocodiles in Australia: the saltwater, with its wider jaw, and the freshwater variety shown above.

152, 153. Creatures of the earth, real or imagined, form a basic part of Aborigines beliefs. They are depicted in rock carvings, cave paintings, sketches done on bark, even the urban murals of today. The modern version, painted on a city wall, features the Rainbow Serpent. The far older rock painting from Nourlangie Rock, Kakadu Park, depicts a god-like ancestor called Lightning Man.

154. Huge galleries of rock paintings, such as these at Kakadu, are part of Aborigine culture. They record the ancestral beings that came to the land and walked over it, singing it to life. Behind them they left their images, records of their passing. Down through the ages the paintings have been retouched to keep them alive. Even today this is done, using red and yellow ochres, clays and charcoal, colours and materials from the earth to which all creatures, great and small, belong.

155, 156. Most Aboriginal rock paintings are of living creatures, reptiles, marsupials, birds, fish, the prime movers of the Dreamtime. Human figures also appear, some with spears or stone axes, taking part in the hunt for food. Other fragile stick-like creatures dance and sing, run lightly over the land. Some are wounded, speared themselves, as if the earth had turned against them. The earliest Aboriginal images on stone were made about 20,000 years ago in Koonalda Cave, South Australia; they are among the oldest in the world.

157. Kangaroos, sometimes in X-ray presentation, with the animal's bones showing through, are frequent features of Aboriginal art. The kangaroo was one of the prime movers of the Dreamtime, one of the ancestral beings that brought the earth to life. Myths exist of kangaroo skins being thrown on the land and turning into lakes. Tales are told of clouds of kangaroos arriving in thunderous storms that uprooted the rocks themselves. When the fierce winds had gone, the kangaroos came down to the earth and began to reshape it, creating the face it presents today.

gouged out river beds, settled down one night to sleep. The snake's power was so great that, even asleep, it turned the sandhill it lay by into a massive mountain of rock. The legend of Uluru, and many others like it, belongs to the Aborigines' Dreamtime, the time of creation, the bonding of man to the land.

The Dreamtime, from which the Songlines issued, was when creative ancestral beings such as the rainbow serpent, Wilkuda the Hunter, the creator of the kangaroo, and Barramundi, the father of fish, walked the land, marked out its features, and brought to life all things that lived in the country now known as Australia, the Aborigines included. The songs the creative ancestors sang, the designs they painted on the rocks and on themselves, continue into the living present. There is no past or future in the Dreamtime, all is one continuous present, which changes perhaps, with alterations of space and time, but part of a living whole.

It is said that the Aboriginal totem ancestors sang the land into existence, then lifted their voices to bring to life the shapes they dreamed of, the beings they wanted to walk their earth. Songs passed down through countless generations recount the power, the magic, of the First Fathers of the country that were given breath. So it may not seem surprising to many Aborigines today that now their voices have been raised once more, a new Dreamtime is with them, or that a new cycling of the old, ever-present fathering of the land has been placed in their custodial hands.

Aboriginal art, the only graphic record of their creative myths and legends, is today valued for what it is: the story of creation seen through the Aborigines' eyes. It is the world's oldest continuous living art; much of it is the same as the earliest Australian rock engravings that go back twenty thousand years. Totem animals and birds, the possum, the crocodile, the mullet have been painted again and again in traditional ways, often skeletal in appearance, with the bones showing through.

Perhaps, however, the most celebrated Aboriginal voice recently has been that lifted by the pop group Yothu Yindi whose hit *Treaty* was Australia's favourite song in 1991. Appearing in a mixture of western dress and Aboriginal body paint, and playing a combination of the old and new musical instruments, they symbolise an amalgam of what is past and what is present. Whether you like their music or not, they are part of a vigorous Dreamtime.

The Great, The Glorious

Although many Australians have become famous, have passed into that public realm of household names where they have been looked at, admired and gossiped over, those best known are the performers — the singers, the actors, the dancers. The world is, after all, a stage. And it is a stage that is, quite likely, Australia's best known international feature — the Sydney Opera House.

Long before the Opera House was ever thought of, Dame Nellie Melba, born Helen Mitchell, came into the world. She was the first Australian to win international fame, the wonderful purity of her soprano voice capturing hearts around the world. For her debut in the Brussels Opera House, she adopted the name Melba (she'd been called Nellie all her life) in honour of Melbourne, her native city. From the moment the public heard her voice, at the relatively late starting age of twenty-six, she was an instant success. She sang in all the capitals of Europe, in America, took her own country by storm, and until 1920 was the queen at Covent Garden.

A large lady with a formidable presence, she nevertheless had her softer side. A sweet tooth led to the creation of a peach, raspberry syrup and ice cream dish in her honour, named Peach Melba, still a favourite on the Down Under Christmas table, which is set at the height of the summer sun. When she was made a Dame of the British Empire in 1918 for the money she raised in concerts for the war effort, it is claimed her secretary discovered her dancing naked in her bedroom, happily singing 'I'm a Dame. I'm a Dame.'

Nellie Melba led a long line of Australian singers and performers to international fame. She was followed by Judith Anderson, who in 1948 received the New York Critics' Award for 'the most distinguished actress in the American theatre'. Eileen Joyce was another talented Australian who performed on the grand stages of the world. As a pianist she played with some of the greatest conductors of her time. When he first heard her play, the composer Percy Grainger said she was the most transcendentally gifted child he had ever heard. Grainger himself was no stranger to fame. Though best known for his tuneful 'Country Gardens', he had a wide-ranging, if eccentric, music career. He experimented with sound combinations and ways of playing instruments that were less than conventional — hammers used on piano keys, for example, or organ notes held down by the nose.

Another somewhat eccentric and greatly talented Australian was Robert Helpmann, knighted in 1968 for his distinguished contribution to ballet and choreography. Helpmann danced, sang, acted and entertained people all over the world, but his greatest contribution to the theatre was in ballet. In 1933 he was accepted into the Sadler's Wells Ballet School, soon joined the company itself and, almost as rapidly, became its leading male dancer. It is said that, when given the opportunity to choose a junior lead by Ninette de Valois, the company's director, he picked out a girl named Peggy Hookham. She went on to become Margot Fonteyn. Later in life Helpmann went into films and seemed to enjoy whatever he did. When making *55 Days in Peking*, he sent a postcard to a friend saying it was all 'lots of fun' but they were making him up to look like 'Yul Brynner's grandmother'.

There is a long line of Australian film stars, actors and actresses who have dashed energetically on, and off, the screen. Errol Flynn was, throughout the 1930s and 1940s, one of Hollywood's leading men, playing impudently, with a certain swagger that cinemagoers loved. Flynn was followed to Hollywood by actors like Keith Michell, Rod Taylor, Leo McKern, Mel Gibson and Paul Hogan, all men who acted vigorously, carrying with them

The Public Museum and Library, Melbourne, 1880

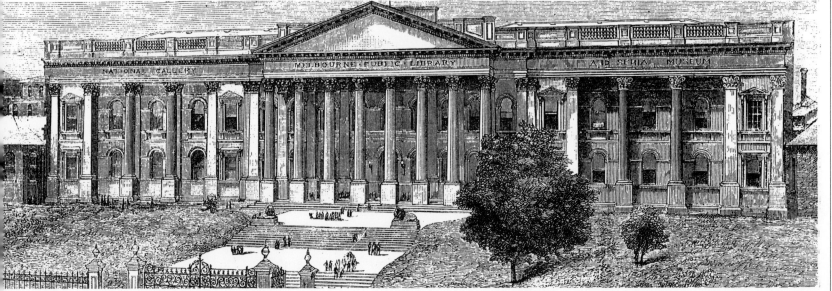

something of the pioneer, the strongman, the Outback voice. On the opera stage, Nellie Melba's place has been taken by other Australian women, most notably Joan Sutherland, who has triumphed all over the world. In the field of pop music, there have been Helen Reddy, Olivia Newton-John and, more recently, Kylie Minogue, a multimillionaire at the age of twenty-two, about the same age that Melba was when she took her first serious singing lessons.

In Australia itself, film-making has had a curious history. It is claimed that the world's first full-length film was Australian — a biblical epic called *Soldiers of the Cross* — made in 1900 for the Salvation Army. It didn't win any prizes, but it was a start: some ninety more feature films were made before 1914. Then the First World War and, later, the need for sound set the industry back. For years it struggled, having like Hollywood plenty of space and natural light, but lacking funds and talent. In 1970, when the Australian voice was being lifted strongly, a government body, the Australian Film Development Corporation, was established to provide grants, investment and encouragement for the film industry. A new wave of Down Under movies, actors and directors appeared.

Between 1970 and 1980 over one hundred and fifty feature films were made with government assistance and out of the climate of the time came some of the best-known and most successful directors in films today. It is both a pity and a mark of their value that many of them are now better known in Hollywood than in Australia. Peter Weir is one such. Weir became famous outside his own country for *Picnic at Hanging Rock*, a beautiful, moody film about the disappearance of a group of schoolgirls in 1900. Later, in America, Weir made the very successful *Witness*, and more recently *Green Card* with Gerard Depardieu, a film he wrote, produced and directed. Bruce Beresford is another Australian director who went overseas to further fame after his *Breaker Morant* won several Australian Academy Awards. So too did George Miller after his *Mad Max* series launched himself and Mel Gibson on their remarkably successful ways.

While Australian film-makers were bursting onto the international scene, the final act of another drama was being played out on a tongue of land known as Bennelong Point in Sydney Harbour, where the Opera House was being built. The dream of an opera house resting above the waters of the harbour, nested beneath the arch of the bridge, is credited to Eugene Goossens, resident conductor of the Sydney Symphony Orchestra in 1954, when the plan was first discussed. It took twenty years to complete.

An international competition was held in search of a design. Like that for the city of Canberra, nearly half a century earlier, it was won by a foreigner, the Dane Jorn Utzon, whose brilliant piece of conceptual fantasy, based on shell forms, undulating creatures of the deep, overriding curls of waves, seemed to be just what the planners wanted. Here was a symbol of Australia's refound sense of nationality, an expression of the newly-lifted voice. The only problem was that no-one, the architect included, appeared to have any idea how to build the dream palace or what it would eventually cost.

For six years the structural engineering firm of Ove Arup struggled to find a way the huge multi-curved roof could be put up without immediately falling down. No tested structural technology existed to handle the stresses, the strains, the towering forces that Utzon's design demanded. Nothing quite as complicated as the interior halls, the stages with their multi-functional uses, the auditoriums, the cinemas, the rest-rooms and cafeterias seemed ever to have been put together before. As the engineers toiled, the price rose. Refusing to accept modifications, Utzon resigned from the project and returned to Denmark, to the little town near Elsinore he came from. Elsinore, although the matters are unrelated, is where Shakespeare's Hamlet saw his father's ghost, the vision that sent him mad.

One bright star that remained on the horizon was the Opera House Lottery. As expenditure rose, more tickets were sold, the profits going to foot the ever-increasing bill. In the end, the building cost one hundred and two million Australian dollars, a fair step up from the originally estimated twelve. However, built it was — fourteen years after Ove Arup and his men finally worked out how. The original plans were modified, mainly in the interior, by a team of Australian architects, but the roof structure remained much the same — a cluster of eloquent sound cones of the future, or a heap of broken egg-shells, depending on your point of view. On October 20, 1973, Queen Elizabeth II opened the Sydney Opera House, a building that might be one of the world's last great architectural follies, standing beside the Taj Mahal or the Sphinx in its glory.

After the opening, in the soft Australian October night, there was a display of fireworks that lit up the whole of Sydney's splendid harbour, throwing its light onto the great grinning face of Luna Park that lies nestled diagonally opposite, beneath the other end of the Harbour Bridge. There, with its giant Ferris wheel, its Big Dipper, its stands for hot-dogs, pop-corn and candy-floss, the old amusement park might well have been wondering, as its laughing face grew brighter in the rockets' glow, who might be called the bigger joke, who might be called the fool.

Perhaps the last word in the Australian voice should go to Barry Humphries, whose performances as Dame Edna Everage — Strine for Average — have delighted audiences wherever 'she' has appeared. Dame Edna, bustling on stage ludicrously overdressed, beaming from behind her 1940s spectacles, satirises Australian suburbia with a sizzling and endearing accuracy. Gushing gossip and criticism, praise and condemnation, Dame Edna can be wildly funny and, in the same moment, touch something close to the heart.

Humphries has a clear eye that sees strength and weakness, side by side, in the independent Down Under islander, the strangely self-deprecating creature with a continental spirit.

University College, Melbourne, 1880

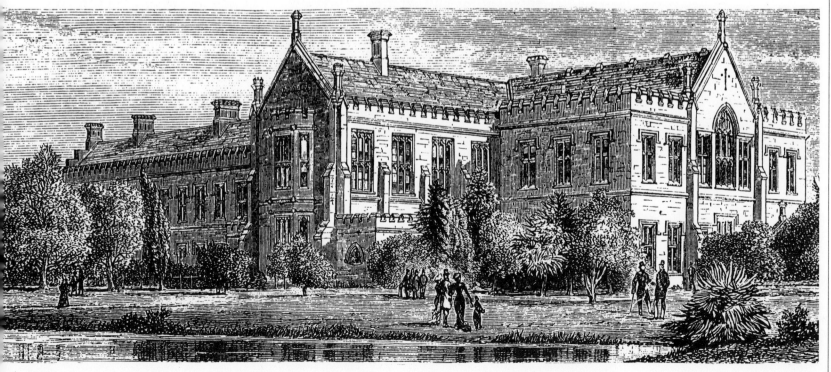

GOVERNMENT

The Policy Makers

Australia's first federal government, formed after the colonies came together to create one nation in 1901, was an odd coalition voted in piecemeal yet dealing with the country as a whole. In the House of Representatives, the lower house, similar to the British House of Commons, the Protectionist Party won the most seats — but not enough to give it control. An alliance was formed with the Labor Party and the coalition was headed by Edmund Barton, Protectionist leader, the first Prime Minister of Australia. The same alliance controlled the Senate, the upper house, a body designed to review proposed legislation.

The Protectionist Party has long since disappeared, although the two-house system remains. Under the Commonwealth Act that set the process in motion, the British monarch was head of state. This, too, continues down to the present: the Queen is the country's titular head, but not as Queen of England; she is there in her capacity as Queen of Australia. This, however, may be due to change. Recent moves have been made toward Australian independence from the British Crown. In 1992 it was decided that when allegiance to Australia was declared in official ceremonies, it was not to include allegiance to the Queen.

Edmund Barton, first Prime Minister, did not last long. He retired just over two years after his government took office, but he saw into law three of Australia's most significant pieces of early legislation. One gave all women the right to vote — the first government had been voted into office mainly by men, most states having refused women the franchise. Another legislative move was to introduce a national customs tariff on imported goods. A quarter of the money raised by this went to the federal government, the rest was distributed to the states — as the old colonies were now referred to. But the most determined bill of all was the Immigration Restrictions Act, the White Australia Policy as it came to be known, although never officially called by such a name.

Australia had long been frightened of foreign immigration. Chinese sifting through old gold workings had made early colonists aware of competition from the north. Pacific Island natives cutting Queensland sugar cane for little money, sometimes not much more than their keep, had given white labour a sense of what life might be like if they were challenged for their jobs. In fact, to placate the sugar growers for the loss of their cheap labour, a Sugar Bounty Act was introduced in 1903 to pay a bounty on sugar-cane — provided it was cut by white labour. Thus, Edmund Barton, though not long in office, left behind him an Australia that was to be white-skinned, economically protected against imported foreign goods, and politically pragmatic — his coalition with the Labor Party had given him what he wanted.

The White Australia Policy had a remarkably limiting effect on the urbanisation of the country. After the gold rushes in the middle of the nineteenth century when population growth boomed, the number of immigrants steadied. They continued to arrive, but at a slower rate and mostly from the British Isles. In 1914 Australia had a population of just under five million, ninety-five per cent of whom were of British descent. By the mid-1940s the number of Australians had grown to only seven million and the Labor Prime Minister of the day, Joseph 'Ben' Chiefley, and his Cabinet realised that Australia needed people. 'Populate or perish' became the government's slogan. An agreement was reached with the British government over assisted passages for those wishing to come to new prospects Down Under. Like similar assistance some one hundred years earlier, 'bounty' passages were made available to ex-servicemen and their families, who paid nothing at all, and others, who had to contribute ten pounds toward their fare.

But Australia needed more and looked further afield. Refugees from Europe, usually selected for their blond hair, blue eyes, unmistakably Nordic look, were brought into the country at the Australian government's expense. And the population began to grow again — in spite of protests from trade unions alarmed that their jobs might go to workers who would do them for less — the ghosts of the Kanakas, as the Islanders who worked in their sugar fields were called, walked the land again.

Yet the White Australia Policy continued to bite into the nation's soul. Asians remained on the not-wanted list. Part of this discrimination is understandable. Australian soldiers, captured by the Japanese in World War II, suffered badly. Some were able to forgive, but few to forget. However, anti-Asianism extended beyond the Japanese to everyone from the North. Arthur Caldwell, Australia's Immigration Minister at the time of the 'populate or perish' campaign, remarked — not entirely in jest, as far as many Australians were concerned — 'Two Wongs do not make a White.' There was also discrimination within Australian society. Before World War II nearly eighty per cent of the country were Church of England or other Protestants, and the rest Catholics, mainly Irish in descent. Only a scattering of the other religions were practised and their followers were not entirely popular. As a result, Jews were not allowed to become members of the Melbourne Stock Exchange until the 1960s, and many Catholics found their applications turned down when they tried to become members of exclusive country clubs.

However, as immigrants began pouring into Australia at the end of the 1940s, tolerance for skin colour, foreign accents, different beliefs grew. Even those from the Near Asian North were allowed entry. This in part was an attempt to placate Australia's trading partners, increasingly more important since Britain's entry into the European Economic Community, foremost among whom was Japan. By the 1980s, nearly one third of all immigrants were Asian, and they were proving, as they have done elsewhere in the world, what good citizens they are.

While the country was broadening as a whole, the power bases of the political parties were narrowing, becoming more deeply entrenched. The man most responsible was Robert, later Sir Robert, Menzies who was Prime Minister twice, the first time between 1939 and 1941, and the second for a much longer period, from 1949 to 1966. As leader of the United Australia Party, Menzies first took over the Prime Minister's office at a time of intense political in-fighting. Europe was on the verge of another conflict that was to become the Second World War and Australia lacked positive leadership, firm party lines for the country to follow.

In the years leading up to 1939 there had been coalitions, combinations of various political groups, a changing of partners that had left the voter confused. Australia had suffered badly in the Great Depression, in the years of hunger, 1931 and 1932. As it emerged from the 'Slump', it faced political confusion. A new Country Party had emerged. The old Liberal Party had joined forces with the National Labor Party. Menzies himself left the Australian Labor Party to join, in combination with the old Nationalist Party, a new United Australia Party. All in all, the country's lack of experience in federal politics was showing through badly.

In the general election of 1931, the United Australia Party was voted into power. It was led by Joseph Lyons, who held the party together until he died in office and Robert Menzies emerged from the leadership battle as Prime Minister of Australia. He was, however, very unpopular. He was accused by his political enemies of having avoided military service, an accusation that has curious parallels in the United States today. He was also known as Pig Iron Bob because his government had permitted the exportation of pig iron — crude iron including scrap — to Japan. Dock workers refused to load the metal onto cargo ships, claiming that if Japan came into the war, now begun in Europe, the material might be returned in the shape of bombs or shells. In the end, unable to hold together his fragile coalition, which depended on the support of two Independent members of the House of Representatives, Menzies resigned as Prime Minister. Just over a month later his government was defeated by a motion of no-confidence and the Labor Party became the government of the day.

For eight years Menzies remained in opposition. The war years and those that followed saw Australia in Labor's hands. John Curtin took over as prime Minister from Menzies in 1941 and remained in that office until he died in 1945. He was a tall, grey man with steel-rimmed spectacles, somewhat bleak in appearance, a 'secular saint' was what one historian called him. Curtin was a reformed alcoholic and once confessed that when he drank it was to share the 'humanity of fellowship' — an honest realisation of why men and women, not only in Australia, turn to alcohol to unlock barriers within.

Curtin was equally forthright about Australia's position during the Second World War. The Japanese, whom he called 'short-sighted, underfed and fanatical', were close to invading the country. Darwin in the north had been bombed, and Sydney shelled from submarines. Curtin realised that the defence of Australia depended on the United States much more than on the United Kingdom. He disputed a number of Churchill's decisions and welcomed General Douglas MacArthur when the Americans moved their headquarters from the Philippines to Melbourne. In many ways Curtin's government was a turning point in Australia's history, moving it from its old English 'Home' toward a new alliance with the United States.

On his death, Curtin was replaced by Ben Chiefley, the man who advocated a 'populate or perish' strategy as the only way of making Australia strong. For a while things went well for Chiefley: the war had come to an end, and despite the number of immigrants, there seemed to be work for all. The Australian Labor Party, with its roots in the trade unions, was strong. Chiefley, a determined socialist, believed that the wealth of the country belonged to all. He also believed in nationalisation of some of Australia's industries and this, in the end, led to his downfall. His move to nationalise the airlines, particularly Quantas, was successful, but when he turned to banking, the country protested. He was supported by the Communist Party and that did not help. He was opposed not only by the banks but also by the newspapers, which presented Menzies and his newly-formed Liberal Party — a realignment of some fourteen separate political factions — as the saviour of the time. Menzies' 'Pig Iron' phase was forgotten and he became Prime Minister for the second time in 1949.

By 1949 Menzies had matured considerably. He was a level-eyed, beetle-browed man in his fifties with grey hair and a statesmanlike appearance. He was also very conservative in his politics, opposed the strength of the trade unions, Chiefley's socialism, and went so far in his campaign promises as to say that he would ban the Communist Party once he was in power. This he attempted to do and even succeeded in getting a bill to that effect through both houses of parliament. However the Communist Party and ten unions appealed to Australia's High Court and the act was finally declared invalid as it infringed civil liberties.

This did not stop Menzies in his course as Australian Prime Minister of the century. He saw Australia through the Korean War and into the ANZUS Treaty, a pact with New Zealand and the United States under

158. Mustering in Cape York, Queensland, where holdings are so large they are measured in thousands of square miles. Other states have cattle-stations just as vast: Western Australia and the Northern Territory raise huge herds for export. Annual production of beef and veal ranges from 1.3 to 2 million tons, two-thirds of which is exported to more than a hundred countries throughout the world, with the USA and Japan the largest customers.

which the Pacific area would enjoy the protection of the three countries involved. Menzies was looking for powerful friends and the U.S.A. was the most powerful of all.

In 1956 the Olympic Games were held in Melbourne in a climate far from politically calm. Spain and the Netherlands refused to send teams in protest against the Soviet invasion of Hungary. The Chinese did not turn up because Taiwan was to be represented there. Lebanon and Egypt were not there either because of what was happening in the Middle East. And when the Hungarian and Soviet teams played against each other in a water polo match, the water became red with blood. Finally, several Romanian and Hungarian team members defected. On the sporting side, the Games were a triumph for the hosts, especially Australian swimming stars, among them Dawn Frazer and Lorraine Crap, whose names passed into Olympic history. Australia came third in the overall medal table, behind the Soviet Union and the United States, proving once again what a splendidly athletic nation it can be when it really tries.

One of the last acts that Menzies saw through parliament before he retired, at the age of seventy-one, was that which changed Australia's currency to a decimal system. Decimal currency was an old issue. It had first been recommended in 1902, when the first Federal Parliament met. Nothing, however, was done. Nor was any action taken in 1937 when decimalisation was again proposed. In 1957, when it came up again, Menzies was not in favour. His heart belonged, in many ways, to England, to the old system, to the British-based pounds, shillings and pence. In fact, when finally convinced that the decimal mode would benefit the business community and was much more suited to the computer age, he wanted to call the main unit the 'royal'. Public protest made him select the more popular 'dollar'.

When Robert Gordon Menzies retired in 1966 he had been in politics for some thirty-seven years, nearly twenty of them as Prime Minister. For many Australians he embodied the country himself; he was intelligent; he was a battler; he saw his land as part of the British Empire. His loyalties to Crown and country were beyond question. He was also the only really towering figure to emerge from Australia on the world's political stage.

After Menzies

The political gap that Menzies left was filled by lesser men. Although accused of being arrogant, sometimes bullying, Menzies had a presence that extended beyond Australia's shores. Those who followed seemed puppets by comparison, shell-men acting out a role. In the six years that followed Menzies' seventeen-year term, Australia had three Prime Ministers. The first was Harold Holt. More media-conscious, more media-appreciative than Menzies had ever been, he was often photographed on the beach with bikini-clad companions. But he was far less accomplished on the political scene. He embarrassed a number of Australians by loudly declaring on a visit to the United States in 1966 that he would go 'All the way with LBJ' in support of the American President's Vietnam policy. Holt, like Menzies, believed that Australia should be involved in the Vietnam War, but it was Holt who faced the public outcry when the war became so unpopular in the mid-1960s.

In Holt's election year, 1966, President Lyndon Johnson visited Australia in support, and although security was tight demonstrators splashed Johnson's car with paint in Melbourne. In Sydney protesters lay

*159, 160. When the English came to
Australia they brought their horses with
them as farm animals, transport, creatures
to race. Perth, where this horse farm rests
in quiet countryside, was eagerly settled by
Englishmen who dreamed of creating a
landscape-from-home on the far side of the
world. In the beginning, before any racetracks existed, they galloped their horses
along Fremantle beach. Today the tradition
continues: Perth has two flat-racing courses and two night-trotting tracks.*

161. Some horses escaped or were set free, and became wild. In Australia they are known as brumbies, from the Aborigine word 'booramby', meaning untamed. Brumbies wander the grasslands where they can roam free, but often they are hunted, shot down for so-called sport, and used for dog food. This is particularly the case in Queensland, where farmers are inclined to shoot anything that competes for forage with their stock. At times they employ professional hunters to rid themselves of rabbits, dingoes, kangaroos and wild horses.

162, 163. Cape York Peninsula, one of the most-varied, least populated farming tracts in Australia. It ranges from dry Outback stations, where cactus grows and all that seems to be alive is the buzzing of flies, to jungle-like tropical rain forest, fern-clad, impenetrable, where pythons lie silently on branches in the soft wet air. There are river beds in rocky landscapes that one day are completely dry and the next raging torrents. Through billowing Cape York dust our mustering horseman rides, his dog beside him, his eyes on the track ahead — you never know what to expect in this part of Australia.

164. Under a low and heavy sky the broad
sweep of Clare Valley unfolds 80 miles
north of Adelaide, South Australia. Settled
in 1842 and named after Ireland's County
Clare, the valley has become one of the
great producers of Australian wine, especially high-quality white wines, a branch of
the country's viticulture that has bloomed
in recent years. South Australia makes
more than half of Australia's wine and
most of it has found respect among wine-
tasters everywhere.

165. Irish Jesuits planted the first grape vines in Clare Valley, at the southern tip of the Flinders Range. The wine they produced was used for Communion. Many others came from Ireland when the colony began, some as convicts, others as free men, and a certain few added their names to early Australian legend. The most famous of these was Ned Kelly, bushranger, who died young, shot down by the law.

166, 167. A country farmhouse in wood or stone, gum trees, sun-baked grasses — elements frequently encountered on the outskirts of towns around Australia's Civilised Rim. Most Australians inhabit the long strip down the east coast or the south-west corner. Only 15 per cent of the population (approaching 18 million) live in rural areas.

168. Broad pasturelands, a lifting hillside, widely-cast clumps of trees — the empty landscape rolls away. The belief that Australia would provide endless pine trees, needed as masts and spars for sailing ships of the time, was one of the reasons the land was chosen as a penal settlement. Trees there were and, like elsewhere in the world, they were cut down and not replaced. Miles of deforested countryside resulted, thin pasture, hillsides covered with scrub. Only now are trees being replanted. By the year 2000 it is hoped there will be a billion more growing in Australia.

169, 170. Australia's love of horses, especially the racing kind, is best exemplified by Phar Lap, a legend in his time. Bred in New Zealand, raced in Australia, Phar Lap won the Melbourne Cup in 1930. In 1932 the champion was taken on a tour of international racetracks. After winning in New Mexico he suddenly died and no one discovered why. Such is the stuff of which myths are made. The whole country mourned. Poems were written, songs were sung. The great horse's hide, heart and skeleton were carefully preserved and are now on display in various museums.

*171, 172. The Barossa and Clare Valleys,
South Australia, where much of Australia's
best wine comes from, owe their beginnings to religious settlements, albeit of different faiths. The Barossa vineyards (overleaf) were established by German
Lutherans, those at Clare (pp. 198-199) by
Irish Catholics. In both cases their descen-
dants have become masters of the grape.
First efforts, however, were of dubious
quality. Then the gold rushes of the 1850s
gave local products a boost. Thirsty diggers with cash to spare would drink anything, and shout for more. Today, the wine
is finer, but the demand is just as great.*

173. *Oriental hats protect Asian workers against Australian sun as they harvest a field near Perth. In the early days Asian 'coolies', mainly Indian and Chinese, were imported as labour. Later, when the gold rushes drew fossickers, more Chinese came. The Japanese began a pearling industry in the western north. Soon Australia became nervous about its non-white workers, who toiled long hours for little pay. Finally a White Australia immigration policy kept them away. Only in the past decade have they been given the same chance as anyone else.*

174. From this sugar-cane plantation, and others like it, comes a great lump of the world's raw sugar. In a giant swathe, running down from north Queensland to New South Wales, Australian sugar-cane sucks sweetness from the earth, the sun, the tropical air. When harvested, cane is burned to drive away snakes and hornets, cut and then taken to the mill. The sugar is consumed domestically or exported. Waste fibre is used as fuel. Molasses, the cane juice before sugar crystallises out, becomes stock food or is turned into rum. Very little of the harvest goes to waste.

175, 176. They stretch across the countryside like a moving cloud, which is how the Aborigines described them when they first set eyes on sheep. 'Jumbuck', the word they used, passed into the language, and is the central theme of 'Waltzing Matilda', Australia's unofficial national anthem. The sheep that arrived with the First Fleet, however, were scraggy, goat-like creatures, raised for meat, not for wool. Today, the country is the world's second largest exporter of mutton and lamb, and first in the export of live sheep.

177. Australia is the world's major grower of fine wool, producing a third of the total. The merino, introduced in the 1790s, makes up 80 per cent of the country's flock. New South Wales is the main wool-growing state, Western Australia comes second. Of all the wool cropped, 97 per cent is exported, bringing in some $ 6000 million a year.

178. A rolling sea of golden grain. Wheat grows in all states except the Northern Territory. Western Australia produces most. The country rates third in the world as exporter of wheat. Whichever way you cut it, that adds up to a lot of bread.

179, 180. At one time it was said that the nation lived off the sheep's back, but although wool is still the largest money earner, other products have become increasingly important. Beef ranks second to wool, wheat runs third. Others, such as cotton and sugar, are valuable contributors to the nation's purse. And Australia virtually feeds itself, supplying 95 per cent of its domestic needs.

181. Although farmers have invested fortunes in machinery to till, sow and harvest the land, some processes remain as their forefathers knew them. This windmill on a Clare Valley farm still raises water from the ground, working as the winds decide. Here, in pleasant, fertile South Australia, where some of the nation's most fruitful earth is turned, it is nice to see that certain elements remain unchanged, and function as well now as they did in the past.

182. Cattle on the move in Queensland, the largest beef-producing state on the continent, where 40 per cent of the national herd is raised. North Australian cattle pastures were discovered in the mid-1800s by explorers hoping to win a cash prize, offered by the South Australian government, for the first south-north crossing of the country. Burke and Wills were the first men to arrive at the northern coast. They became heroes but, sadly, starved to death on the return journey. Cattlemen followed in their footsteps and opened up the land. They were the men who won the real prize.

183. Cattle is always moving at the Top
End of Australia. The greatest cattle drive
of all took place in the Northern Territory
in 1942. Australia was at war, Singapore
had fallen, Darwin had been bombed.
There was real fear of a Japanese invasion.
To deprive the invaders of readily available
food, more than 100,000 head of beef were
driven south, travelling in some cases more
than a thousand miles. This mustering
stockman would not have been with them,
but his father may have taken part in the
biggest round-up in the country's history.

184. Not all cattle is moved by mounted
horsemen in the vast pasture lands of
northern Australia. Our stockman, having
brought his herd to the yard, may see it
loaded onto huge road-trains, giant trucks
that speed across the countryside taking
beef to market. These monolithic over-
landers often travel by night, avoiding the
heat, to reduce the number of deaths in
transit. Even so, at most destinations there
are 'Dead on Arrival' pits where carcasses
can be cremated.

185. *Our stockman may have travelled so far with his brood that the only time he sees his boss on the trail is when the man flies in. Mustering can take place over hundreds of miles on cattle stations that are larger than small countries. Grazing is often thin, at times non-existent. Whereas elsewhere in the world acres are evaluated in the number of cattle they support, in parts of Australia calculations are based on the number of acres required to feed a single beast.*

186, 187. Cattle become so spread out on the vast, unfenced pasturelands in the north that there are times when the most efficient way to round them up is by helicopter. It may seem uneconomic to send an expensive aircraft after a lumbering beast, but when stocktime comes and the grass is thin, timing can be critical. Unless the herd is brought in quickly, it may die worth nothing. So helicopters take off, and trucks wait to take the beef to distant markets.

188. Now running smoothly, the herd thunders down, with the drover — a helicopter — weaving above. In the old days mustering was the stockman's task alone. It was done by men as tough and laconic as any Western cowboy. They spent days with their horses, camped out at night, as they nursed their herd to the stockyard. When they reached a town, they took part in rodeos, spent money on wine, women, even song. Country and Western music is called Queensland Opera in this part of the world.

189. The lot of a beast in northern Australia is not to be envied. There are few soft green pastures, no farmer plodding home at dusk. Fodder is sparse, the landscape hard. There are snakes to deal with, flies to drive you mad. Fierce heat can mean that calves born at noon will not survive. Then a helicopter, swirling dust and grasses, thundering down a wall of sound, drives you to the slaughter yard, where you end up as a steak.

down in front of the President's motorcade, an act which prompted the New South Wales Premier to tell the police to 'Run over the bastards'. Fortunately, no one was hurt. Holt won the election, but was not doing well. Scandal and criticism snapped at his heels. One Sunday, in December 1967, high summer Down Under, Harold Holt went for a swim and never returned. He was never seen or heard of again. I was in Australia at the time and I will never forget the sense of disbelief that hung in the air. After Menzies' heavy performance, it seemed impossible that a Prime Minister could have disappeared without a trace.

After a brief caretaker period by the leader of the Country Party, the other partner in the coalition, and several rounds of bitter in-fighting — there were at least seven aspirants for the job of Prime Minister — Holt was succeeded by John Grey Gorton, an even more controversial figure. Gorton gave the impression he was trying to be his own man, independent of the party, the Cabinet, sometimes the country as a whole. At one stage he suggested that his type of isolation could be applied to Australia's defence, that an 'Israeli-type' of defence strategy could be brought into being, that 'fortress Australia' was the name of the game, though how this would be financed and by whom was never made clear.

Gorton also seemed to have a curious bi-focal attitude toward America. At his first press conference, he declared that he was against American use of air power to destroy North Vietnam. Subsequently he said that no more Australian troops would be sent to fight in Vietnam. Yet, later, he told President Nixon, in a heavy-handed attempt at mateyness, that 'We will go a-waltzing Matilda with you,' — a comment that seems to have left Nixon puzzled as to what exactly was meant. And just before his downfall Gorton was criticised for being too closely tied to American policy as far as the war was concerned. After a few minor scandals about his association with certain young ladies and a much more serious matter concerning who was making the decisions in Vietnam, the army or the government, Gorton resigned. He actually voted against himself in the meeting called to discuss his leadership, perhaps feeling he could not continue on his vote alone.

Gorton was followed into office by William McMahon, Prime Minister from 1971 to 1972, the man who led the Liberal-Country Party coalition to defeat after twenty-three years of continuous rule. McMahon was a man in his sixties who seemed tired, as worn out as many in the country thought the government, after Menzies, had become. In the 1972 general election he, the Liberal and the Country Party were swept out of power by a renewed Labor Party led by Edward Gough Whitlam, a man who seemed to represent the new nationalism that was flowing through Australia's veins, the new voice that was being heard country-wide.

The Australian Labor Party had gone through hard times. One of the worst blows against it had been the so-called Petrov affair. Early in 1954 Vladimir Petrov, a third secretary at the Soviet Embassy in Canberra, defected and was granted political asylum in Australia. As the world watched, the Russians attempted to remove Petrov's wife from Australia, presumably to use her to prevent him revealing too many secrets. Bundled onto a Quantas aircraft at Sydney's airport by two heavy-set Russian minders, her face twisted with confusion and grief, Mrs Petrov began her exit from the country. On board, following Menzies' instructions, a flight attendant asked the frightened woman if she was going of her own free will. Mrs Petrov said little, but gave the impression that she would rather be going anywhere else than back to Russian soil. As a result, when the aircraft stopped to refuel at Darwin, the Northern Territory police disarmed the

190. Aircraft play their part in the Australian Outback in many ways. The most famous role of all is in the Flying Doctor Service, begun in 1928 to bring much-needed service to outstations, where an appendicitis was often fatal. Medical advice is always available by radio, but in case of an emergency the doctor flies in, lands on a home-made airstrip, and brings personal attention to the patient.

Russians and gave Mrs Petrov the chance to talk to her husband. She decided to stay and the Petrov's were put into hiding, given new lives to lead.

However, in the course of the Royal Commission, set up to evaluate information given by Petrov to the government in return for asylum, two members of the Labor Party's inner circle were named as possible sources of information given to the Russian Embassy. They were defended by Ewatt, leader of the Labor Party who, although a lawyer by profession and High Court judge, performed ineptly before the Petrov Commission. When he claimed that he had been in touch with Molotov, the Foreign Minister, to ask if the Petrov evidence against the Labor Party members was sound, and that Molotov had denied it was, Ewatt was virtually laughed out of court.

This, in part, led to the Labor Party being branded pro-Communist, and to a division in its ranks which has never been entirely healed. Two cornerstones of the Labor movement, the trade unions and the Catholic Church, shifted apart. A new Labor group, the Democratic Labor Party, came into being. It was anti-Communist and, for a long time, positively anti-Labor as far as the old party was concerned. The result was to make life easier for Menzies year after successful year.

Nevertheless, by the time Menzies' government had run its course, and Gough Whitlam became Prime Minister, the Australian Labor Party was patched together again. Whitlam and his Cabinet stormed into business, making changes on every side. Following what he believed to be the mood of the country, Whitlam began to reform practically everything in sight. A few days after being elected, he abolished conscription, released draft-dodgers who had been jailed, and began the withdrawal of troops from Vietnam. The People's Republic of China was recognised for the first time by Australia, and closer ties were forged with Japan — a step that led to a wave of Asian immigration. Moves were made to grant Papua New Guinea its independence from Australia; apartheid in South Africa was roundly condemned. The Aborigines were to be given back land taken from them when the white men came, especially in the Northern Territory, where seats in the Senate, Australia's upper house, were made available. That and the Capital Territory where Canberra lies were granted two seats each.

This was only the beginning. Tariff barriers were lowered by twenty-five per cent, the Australian dollar was revalued, court appeals to Britain's Privy Council were abolished, sales tax on the contraceptive pill was removed, moves were begun to see that women were paid the same as men, and free legal aid was introduced for those who need it. Whitlam had great plans for the arts and crafts. The Australian Film and Television School, which saw a rebirth of the business, was established under his administration. There was a headiness in the air that reached many Australians living overseas, those who had gone to write or paint or act in Europe or America because they found the climate 'back home' too stifling, too limiting by far. Among them was Germaine Greer, best known for *The Female Eunuch*, one of the great rollers in the wave of feminist writing at the beginning of the 1970s. Greer talked of returning to an Australia where the air was free. She never made it. Whitlam's government found the going too tough to continue. He was stopped in his tracks in 1975.

Part of the problem was the cost of his government's reform. Inflation rose from five to fourteen per cent, money supply was short, and the oil crisis of 1973 did not help him. As well, many Australians were a little frightened by his rate of progress. Before long, much of the country was asking for the headlong pace to slow a little; a breathing space was needed. And while the Labor Party controlled the House of Representatives, they were in a minority in the Senate, which had the power to reject the lower house's legislation. Moreover, the Liberal Party had a new and capable leader, John Malcolm Fraser, a man much more competent than any since the departure of Menzies.

In October 1975 Fraser made a searing attack on Whitlam's government, calling it reprehensible. As a result, he declared, the Senate would not pass the current Budget unless a new election was called for the House of Representatives. A stalemate ensued. The government had no money. And out of the wings, in all his regal glory as representative of the Queen, stepped Governor-General Sir John Kerr, who removed Whitlam from office and installed Malcolm Fraser as caretaker Prime Minister. Kerr justified his actions on the basis that Whitlam, in refusing to call a general election, had violated the Constitution, a fact that has been disputed. However, the result of his action was to change the course of Australian political history. Curiously enough, something similar had occurred in 1931 in New South Wales. Then the Premier, J.T. Lang, was dismissed by the Governor, again because of a financial crisis, although some thought it was because Lang, and not the Governor, be-medalled, in full costume, had opened the Sydney Harbour Bridge.

Once Whitlam was out of office, the Senate passed the Budget bills, then parliament was dissolved and new elections called. These were won by the Liberal-Country Party coalition and Fraser remained in power. During the pre-election period, after the country had cooled down over the Governor-General's switch-around, the voters had time to think. Whitlam had gone too far, too fast was the decision that they came to. Australia settled into another eight years of conservative rule.

The Legacies

Malcolm Fraser inherited an economy that was in something of a mess. Whitlam's men had left inflation high, unemployment was rising, and the unions were strong. Fraser, however, in spite of his campaign vigour, moved relatively slowly once in power. He left many of Labor's reforms in place — the return of land to the Aborigines continued, subsidies to the performing arts went on — but he and his government were handicapped by the financially tough early 1980s. What's more, Fraser's determination to reduce government spending lost him many friends. But he continued, never very popular, criticised by many, holding his position and the country together while much more important events were taking place elsewhere in the world.

These were events that, in one way or another, touched the island-continent drifting in its many seas. In 1977 U.S.-Vietnam peace talks began, and Australian troops were coming home. In 1978 the Camp David peace talks between Egypt and Israel began. Then the Russians invaded Afghanistan and, in Iran, the Ayatollah Khomeini came to power. The cold war's temperature rose, the Middle East became a boiling point, and citizens in Australia wondered where the price of oil would go and how it would affect their purse. In 1981 Prince Charles married Lady Diana and millions of Australians wiped their eyes before their TV sets. And, about the same time, the United States found a new president in an old cowboy and Australia began to think of political change.

During the Fraser years, the Labor Party had reorganised, regrouped and found fresh faces. The freshest, certainly in terms of federal politics, was Robert James Lee Hawke, who had been president of the Australian Council of Trade Unions before winning a seat in the lower house of parliament in 1979. A tall, silver-haired man with a heavily handsome face, Hawke was elected leader of the Labor Party the day the 1983 elections were called, elections that the resigning leader, Bill Hayden, said were so right for the Labor Party that any opposition leader could win, even a 'drover's dog'.

Hawke won a landslide victory and came into office with plans to make Australia less dependent on overseas ties, for the country to have its own voice in the Pacific. Like New Zealand, Australia wanted to see the south-west Pacific a nuclear-free zone. However, no ties were broken with the United States, and when American nuclear-armed vessels entered the area, Australia sided with the U.S.A., leaving New Zealand out in the cold. Hawke also kept strong the trading alliance between his country and Japan, even though voices were raised in protest about the 'Asianisation' of Australia.

But the blackest cloud on Hawke's horizon was the gradually worsening world economic situation. Markets everywhere were drawing in; there was no longer the money to buy Australia's minerals, wheat and wool. On top of this, the country's overseas debt was high and the devaluation of the Australian dollar in 1985 did not help. Money men in New York and

On the Yarra Yarra - view from Prince's Bridge, The Melbourne Illustrated, 1880

London, Tokyo and Hong Kong wondered about the country's credit rating and, before long, recession had reached Australia's sunny shore. In 1991 Hawke was out of office.

Bob Hawke's career mirrored in many ways that of the man who held office before him, Malcolm Fraser. Both were Prime Minister for eight years, both were caught in the money-minders' international mill. They were strong, determined campaigners, but neither put through all they hoped to, each leaned heavily on the plans that had been in place when they took over the job. Fraser was a quieter man, somewhat more reserved. Hawke could swing between being what has been called the ocker side of the Australian character, the larrikin, the lair, and something much more gentle, much more revealing of what lay inside. When he wept openly on television while talking about his daughter's drug problems, he touched many Australian hearts. When he was replaced as leader of the Labor Party, and consequently Prime Minister, there were many who were sad to see him go.

Australia's policy-makers, in their many shapes and sizes, political colours and disparate hopes, have made Australia what it is today in less than one hundred years. In 1901, when Australia became a Commonwealth, the population was less than four million. At the beginning of the 1990s it was creeping up toward eighteen million, having more than doubled since 1945. In the past few decades the Aborigine population has increased significantly. It is calculated that by the end of the century it will have reached some three hundred thousand, about the same number as when the white man came in 1788. Immigration has been bringing in approximately one hundred thousand new settlers a year in the last decade, but that has slowed significantly recently. Recession, described at the worst since the end of World War II, has hit the country. The Prime Minister, Paul Keating, who took over from Hawke at the end of 1991, faces problems like those of other leaders in the world. The green shoots of recovery in Australia will be a long time taking root.

Even so, the standard of living in Australia remains high. Some seventy per cent of the population own their own home, about one in every ten with a swimming pool, regardless of the fact that all the large cities are set beside the sea. Almost every second person owns a car, ninety-seven per cent of households have TV sets, most are colour, and an Australian house can hardly be called a home unless it has a refrigerator.

Australia is a highly democratic country. All citizens over the age of eighteen have the right, indeed, the obligation to vote. Their names must be included on the electoral roll and if they fail to vote in a general election, by-election, or referendum to alter the Constitution, they are quite likely to be fined. Likewise, any citizen can stand as a political candidate providing he or she is not a member of the Australian Public Service or the defence forces, an undischarged bankrupt or serving a prison sentence for a year or more. The first two categories can easily sidestep this by resignation; for the last two it is a little more difficult.

Australia is a thriving country, despite present financial problems, which it will certainly overcome. The first time I went to Sydney I was struck by the energy of the city; it has the same electricity that crackles through New York. In many ways the whole nation is equally vital, buzzes with its mix of old and new — those with immigrant roots and those who go back into the colonial past. Australia has an exciting future. It will develop, altering as it goes, adding a little more edge to its engaging character, growing stronger in every respect with the passage of time. It is a country to be proud of.

THE WEALTH OF A NATION

Given by the Earth

From almost the beginning of Australia's colonial history, once the secrets of the soil had been deciphered by the newcomers, after the years of starvation when the early penal settlements almost perished, the country has been good to those who live on its broad and varied surface, beneath its turning skies. It has generally been fruitful, although at times, like some primal god of violent moods, it has turned against its inhabitants. Meteorologists have a name for this turbulent god: they call it the Southern Oscillation.

Most years the weather in Australia is conditioned by the moist warm air that gathers over south-east Asia, that comes down across Indonesia bringing the tail-end of the monsoon to northern Australia and rainfall to most of the rest of the country, except, of course, the hard, dry heart. However, once every five or six years, a ridge of high pressure becomes fixed in place, blocking the normal cycle. This is the Southern Oscillation, which often means that no rain falls, the land under the harsh Australian sun dries and turns into clouds of dust, making conditions right for bush-fires that can sweep destruction across the landscape. Under these terrifying conditions, people, houses, sometimes whole towns are lost, livestock die by the hundreds of thousands, crops are burnt to the ground. And then, as if the primal god is not yet happy with the amount of damage already done, downpours may follow, torrential rains can turn the countryside into miles-square muddy lakes.

In 1983 bush fires in Victoria and South Australia burned some two thousand homes, killed seventy people and destroyed nearly half a million sheep and cattle. In the same year dust storms swept into the city of Melbourne, coming down in dark and swirling clouds and left acres of top-soil covering the streets. In December 1974, Cyclone Tracy almost wiped out the capital of the Northern Territory, Darwin: ninety per cent of the town was flattened and fifty people died. But out of the rubble a new Darwin was built, a brighter stronger place of which the citizens are rightly proud. Though no one would thank Cyclone Tracy it, at least, brought out the best in the people, and showed the world their will and ability to overcome setbacks.

But, in the main, Australia has a blessed climate and the land that is lived on is normally kind and productive. Australia is the world's main producer of fine wool; nearly one third of the world's wool comes from the backs of Australia's sheep. The success of this can be credited to one man, John Macarthur, who with his wife Elizabeth developed the industry in the early days of settlement, when Australia was little more than the colony of New South Wales, land that had not seen a sheep before the white man arrived. Macarthur, sent back to England for fighting a duel with his own colonel when an officer in the Rum Corps, resigned his commission, avoided any harsh penalties, and discovered that English manufacturers were desperate for good wool, as Napoleon's armies had cut off supplies from Spain. So with Spanish merino sheep Macarthur returned to Australia and the wool business began.

By 1822, seventeen years after his return and in spite of being forced to go back to London because of his problems with Captain Bligh, Macarthur was winning medals in England for the quality of the fleece his cross-breed sheep were producing. Since then the wool industry has hardly looked back. Until the 1870s gold, which seemed to turn up wherever anyone looked hard enough, was Australia's most lucrative export. Moreover, the gold rushes took shepherds away from the land and turned many sheep-runs into quagmires, but gradually wool production became the more stable economic branch and in the second half of the nineteenth century turned into the booming business it is today.

Meat production, which in many ways goes hand in hand with wool, brings in one fifth of Australia's export income. Although this is mainly beef and veal, mutton goes to Japan and what used to be the Soviet Union. Live sheep exports, often in converted oil tankers, are increasing, especially to the Middle East, where they are slaughtered according to Muslim ritual. They stream into the giant vessels like ants into a nest.

Stock-men are part of the Australian legend, part of the myth of the Outback: the loner on his horse, his dog trotting beside him through endless clouds of dust. Shepherds, often convict labour with no more than a day's rations at a time — no squatter wanted to give his roustabout any chance to go further than needed — opened up much of the land. As flocks grew and more pasture was required, men and the animals they guarded moved out into the land, following the paths of the great explorers, walking in the footsteps of the Sturts, the Mitchells, the Leichhardts. They lived sheep, they breathed sheep, they ate so much mutton it became known as colonial goose. From them has grown a sort of Australian aristocracy, a 'squatocracy' to some, now tenth-generation Aussies who can be picked out by the clothes they wear: wide-brimmed felt hats, checked sports coats, pale coloured trousers of cavalry twill.

And the stock-man, the drover, the overlander goes on. Today he may not ride a horse but drive a road train, a giant truck with three or four massive trailers towed behind it, carrying up to one hundred cattle or over five hundred sheep. Often travelling at night to escape the heat, they thunder along Outback highways. Some commentators believe that Outback-man is dead, long gone, lost in the swirl of progress, buried under the new waves of immigration, but he seems alive and well. The size of the country sees to that. The in-born sense of curiosity, wanting to know what lies on the far side of every hill, keeps him on his feet. I have hitchhiked over most of western Europe and everywhere I've come across an Australian or two, quite often alone, looking around, seeing what it's like in this part of the world, getting an idea of the place, taking a 'dekko'.

Another kind of Aussie to come out of the vastness of the land, not wearing a sports jacket or clean trousers of cavalry twill, but rather a sweaty black singlet, Australia's version of a vest, and dirty jeans, is the sheep-shearer, the migratory worker who moved from one sheep station to another cutting off the fleece, peeling it off, as Banjo Paterson said. Paterson, and other writers like him, firmly fixed the shearer into the Australian legend; the shearers themselves, with their competitiveness, added to the lustre. All wanted to be the fastest 'gun' in the shearing shed. The world record was set in 1802 by Jackie Howe, he sheared three hundred and twenty-one sheep in one day using hand shears, since mechanical shears were not invented until 1868.

But on the world's commodity markets, Australia is not important only for wool and meat; it ranks third in the world as an exporter of both sugar and wheat. Wheat mountains fill gigantic silos waiting to be sucked away; sugar domes lie sweetly ready to be freighted off; molasses pools sit quietly simmering, soon to be turned into rum.

From the Grape

Hugh Johnson, the British wine-writer, said nearly twenty years ago that one of the very best bottles of red wine he'd ever drunk was Australian. It was a bottle of Rutherglen, and it confirmed his opinion that

191-193. Sunrise or sunset, Ayers Rock is a glorious blaze of reds and vermillions, the flames of the distant sun. It is claimed that no photograph has ever done justice to the sacred stone, to its play of vivid colour. It has to be seen to be believed. Only a fraction of the great rock protrudes above the desert floor. The rest, like an iceberg under water, remains in the earth, unseen. Ayers Rock is part of the same ancient bedding that includes the Olgas, 20 miles away. They are among the oldest sedimentary deposits in the world.

Australia could make some of the world's greatest red wine. Rutherglen in north-east Victoria, near the New South Wales border, was one of the early, best-known wine producing areas in Australia. Then phylloxera struck, the vines died, and it was a long time before Rutherglen recovered. Phylloxera, a green and pink bug, sometimes called the root louse, is the vine-grower's curse. It attacks vine roots in its larval stage, sucking the plant's fluids and causing nodules to develop. Eventually the plant rots and dies. Phylloxera had been in America since time immemorial and vines there built-up a resistance and became immune. When, in the 1870s, it struck Europe, it killed off every vine in sight. In the end, despite the enormity of the task, almost every European vine had to be dug up, American rootstocks planted, and then the European vine grafted onto the phylloxera-resistant base. When the costly little creature finally reached Australia, it attacked Victoria's vines and they too had to be uprooted and American rootstock planted. Other Australian vineyards, through careful control, have escaped. Some of the original vines, planted in the middle of the last century, are still bearing heavily in the Australian sun.

Australia's normally reliable climate, and the fact that vineyards are as far apart as Victoria, Queensland and Western Australia, means that the quality of the country's wines does not vary much according to vintage: all years are similar; most are good. Their quality depends on how the wines are made, not on the amount of sugar in the grape.

Australia's first vines came out with the First Fleet which landed in 1788. Captain Arthur Phillip ceremonially planted them in what is now Sydney's Botanic Gardens, where today a stone wall marks the site of the settlement's first vegetable garden, although nothing celebrates the planting of the colony's original grape. Perhaps it is just as well, for the first wines were quite dreadful and may well have given rise to the unflattering term *plonk*, by which Australian wines were once known, whatever their colour, quality or strength. In any case, wine was not a widely popular drink. The country, after all, had grown out of settlements dominated by rum — another generalisation, given to any hard liquor. Then Australia became a beer-drinking nation, and still is by and large. So wine began as something drunk by the landed gentry, those who had brought the taste for it out with them, not shackled together in the holds of convict ships, but as free men who walked the decks, who believed that what they were developing in Australia was a large corner of a not-altogether-foreign field that would be very much a part of England.

Anthony Trollope, the English novelist who not only published forty-seven novels but also introduced the pillar-box for letters to Britain, had a son who settled in Australia. When Trollope visited him in 1871, he noted how 'meat and wine were served in plenty', although he said nothing about the quality of the plonk. The first vineyards in the old colonies were developed on a commercial scale by John Macarthur who brought out the first merino sheep, fought a pistol duel with his colonel, and fell out with Captain Bligh. It is curious how, in the history of a nation at a certain time, in a certain place, one man rises head and shoulders above all others. Perhaps ambition lifts him, or greed, perseverance, or simple luck. It may have been all of these in the case of John Macarthur but, on one of his enforced exiles from New South Wales, he travelled through France and Switzerland studying the grape. He returned to Australia 'stuffed with information and loaded down with cuttings', as someone said at the time. By 1827 he was producing twenty thousand gallons a year and selling it in Sydney.

Another who helped found the industry was Gregory Blaxland, one of

57-59. Under guldrusherna i Västaustralien vid slutet av 1800-talet expanderade Fremantle snabbt och fick då en del vacker arkitektur som på bilden. Sedan följde en tid av nedgång, men i dag är Fremantle en livlig hamnstad varifrån fårkött, vete och mineral exporteras till hela världen. Denna sida.

60. Perth är huvudstad i Västaustralien och började som en ung engelsmans vision. År 1827 seglade James Stirling uppför Swan River och blev övertygad om att en idealisk bosättning kunde startas på de trädkantade flodstränderna. Han ville kalla den Hesperia därför att han såg aftonstjärnan Hesperus (romerskt namn på planeten Venus) i väster på kvällarna vid den tiden. Det hela förlöpte inte så bra som Stirling trott. Det var svåra tider, kolonisterna fick kämpa för att överleva, man var tvungen att be London om en fångtransport för att få tillräckligt med arbetskraft. Det var först när guld upptäcktes i området som Perth började blomstra.   Ovan.

61. Perth ligger lä... ...kilometer från re... ...områden. Unde... ...si...

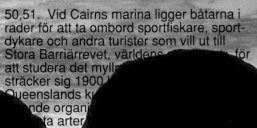

50,51. Vid Cairns marina ligger båtarna i
rader för att ta ombord sportfiskare, sport-
dykare och andra turister som vill ut till
Stora Barriärrevet, världens ████████ för
att studera det myll██████████████████
sträcker sig 1900 █████████████████████
Queenslands k██████████████████████████
██nde organi█████████████████████████████
███ta arter██████████████████████████████
███r, må████████████████████████████████
███havsa█████████████████████████████████
███rev███████████████████████████████████

52. Cairns är Queenslands norra 'huvudstad' och ligger
mellan gröna regnskogar och det blå Stilla havet. En guldrush
under senare hälften av 1800-talet gjorde Cairns känt. I flera
år skeppades tonvis med den gula metallen ut från staden.
Delar av det gamla transportsystemet finns fortfarande kvar i
form av en smalspårig järnväg som gått mellan bergen och
hamnen i gröna tunnlar med ormbunkar. I dag sjuder Cairns
av turistaktiviteter, särskilt i högsäsong från maj till september.
Ovan.

194. Tasmania, or Van Diemen's Land as it was called, was established as a convict settlement in 1803. It was a wild country, damp and unknown, where living conditions were brutal. Its penal colony gained a reputation second only to that of Norfolk Island for inhumane treatment of those imprisoned there. Convict labour built the first houses. Convict hands constructed this bridge at Richmond in 1823. It is the oldest road bridge in all Australia, and still carries traffic across the Coal River.

46. Brisbane ligger bland kullar med tät vegetation. I staden finns bananplantor i trädgårdarna till husen som är byggda på pålar för svalkans skull. Några kilometer utanför staden ligger Mount Coot-tha, varifrån man har fin utsikt över havet och inåt land där man ser Glasshouse Mountains samt floden som slingrar sig emellan. På berget Coot-tha kan man dricka en kopp te medan man njuter av utsikten. T.V.

47. Queensland var en av de sista kolonierna som fick självstyrelse. När kolonin grundades och namngavs 1859 tänkte man på drottning Victoria liksom när kolonin, sedermera staten, Victoria fick sitt namn. När Queensland utvecklades byggdes järnvägen smalspårig. Andra kolonier valde andra spårvidder. Detta fick till följd att passagerarna var tvungna att byta tåg vid resa mellan kolonierna. T.H.

48. Även statyer behöver svalka i Queenslands hetta. På grund av de många soltimmarna har Australien en av de högsta förekomsterna av hudcancer i världen. Solskyddskräm på utsatta delar blir därför allt vanligare.   Ovan.

196–198. Even though it sits in the harsh, dry centre of Australia, a little water trickles constantly from Ayers Rock, as if to say there is life within. The Aborigines certainly believed so. To them the massive stone was Uluru, the spiritual heart of the world. They decorated its caves with paintings, carvings, secret signs. Then the white man took it from them and closed their world. Only in 1985 was Uluru given back to the people to whom it spiritually belongs. Now it is part of a national park where tourists and women of Mutitjulu, the Anangu people, gaze at it together.

49. Floden Brisbane slingrar sig genom staden som en orm. Källan finns i bergen Mowbullan 240 kilometer norrut, men floden är dubbelt så lång på grund av alla krökar. Här vid Kangaroo Point's Story gör floden en sista sväng innan den rinner ut i Stilla havet.   T.H.

199-202. The range of geological wonders found in Australia is fascinating. Some stand like monuments to visitors from a distant world. Here the Pinnacles seem to parade in memory of others who have gone before. Further north the Bungle Bungle Ranges, domed towers striped red, brown and black, brood as if waiting for their masters to return. In the Northern Territory are the Devil's Marbles, enormous playthings 20 feet across. According to Aborigine legend, they are the eggs of the Rainbow Serpent, laid there when the ancestral spirits came down to create the earth.

203. A few hours from sweltering Darwin are the Northern Territory wastelands. Deep in the heart of the rain forest, here, at Sisters Falls, in clear freshwater pools, silver perch flash in the depths, a crocodile may scramble up a bank, and visitors can take a back-to-nature dip.

204-206. Australia's rain forests form a jagged band up the east coast from Tasmania to Cape York. They are wildlife havens, varying from almost impenetrable woods to more open stretches where palms and tree ferns flourish.

the first party to cross the Blue Mountains and gaze out over the rich pasture beyond. In 1825 Blaxland shipped some three hundred gallons of wine to London and won a gold medal — but not for quality. It seems the prize, awarded by the Society for the Encouragement of the Arts, Manufactures and Commerce, was a reward for trying rather than result, intended to encourage the lads on the far side of the world. One of the problems was that, while the grapes grew well, no one had any experience of actually making wine. In an effort to overcome this, the British government sent to Sydney two French prisoners of war, believing that being French wine-drinkers they must know how the stuff was made. They continued drinking in the colony but contributed little toward an improvement in quality. This did not happen until the gold rushes of the 1850s brought new immigrants to the land, among them a number of Frenchmen, Spaniards and Germans who really knew the trade. After that, a better brew began to flow from wineries all over Australia.

The gold rushes, however, had a dual effect, contributing to the ups and downs, the roller coaster of success and failure, that have accompanied the Australian wine business through its varied history. While the gold-seekers had among their number few good viticulturists, there were many thousands more whose uncritical palates and eager throats were prepared to accept anything once they had a few pounds to spare. As a result 'bush wineries' sprouted like mushrooms after rain; sly-grog shops, as unlicensed premises were called, were to be found wherever there were customers. The plonk they sold was often called port or sherry or even Madeira, and though it bore little resemblance to those noble products, few of their customers were critical. These were times when one lucky digger was seen to put a five pound note between two pieces of bread and eat it like a sandwich.

By the 1870s, just when the first flushes of gold fever had subsided and the new settlers were finding work in the towns or on the land, when the wine producers were restoring some of the old standards to their brews, in flew phylloxera to destroy many of the vines. Another down-turn hit the business and it was a long time before it really made a come-back. Phylloxera, in spite of the work involved, was relatively simply handled. A much more serious problem involved the marketing of Australian wines in England, where consumers were used to the light flavour of French burgundies and clarets, light, that is, compared to the heavy robustness of the Australian product. In an effort to overcome this, importers sold Australian brews as tonic wines, rich in iron, suitable for invalids, old ladies beside the fire. It was not a clever move. Sometimes they were blended with South African wines, or those from Cyprus, and very soon were given names like Boarding-house Burgundy, or even worse, and avoided by any drinker with any taste at all. Bought for their alcoholic content and little more, they became standard at student parties or with the winos on the block.

That opinion of Australian wines lasted well into the present century. Then the turmoil in Europe during World War II helped the market Down Under, where consumption of the local product increased threefold. With increased production, this time around, quality also rose. By the 1960s Australian wines had become respectable both at home and abroad. Nowadays they are sought after, especially the best, though a great deal of the finest never leaves Australia's shores. Knowledgeable and appreciative Aussies never let it out of sight. A lot of it, especially the reds, is rich, full and robust. And often robustly described. Instead of something elegant such as 'an interesting little number with an amusing aftertaste', an Australia red from the Hunter Valley, as Hugh Johnson notes, might be

207. An almost perfectly formed coral island emerging from the sea. Green Island, out from Cairns, where snorkellers dive among brightly coloured fish, is a fine example of the landforms corals make. Coral polyps live and die. When their calcareous skeletons build up to reach the surface of the sea, a lagoon forms and is filled with sand. Coconuts are washed ashore, birds bring seeds, some take root and, in time, soil is formed. And another tree-clad island takes its place in the living chain.

241

referred to as having the character of a 'sweaty saddle' or even 'a bloody kangaroo'. In the latter case, quite obviously, the reference is to one of the Big Reds, the Outback Bounders, lords of the open plain.

In the past decade Australian wine making has really taken off. White wine sales in the country itself have soared. Good publicity, intelligent marketing and, above all, improved technology have lifted white wine sales to something like ten times more than in the 1970s. And the trend goes on. Overall, there may be better wines in Europe, but in terms of value for money Australian wines are almost impossible to beat. And the future is bright. By the year 2000 there should be even more bloody great kangaroos bouncing along the skyline.

Under the Crust

Not only gold has come from beneath the surface of the Australian earth; oil, coal, natural gas, other metal-ores and diamonds have been mined from the continent's crust. What is more, some of the oldest rocks in the world are laid bare on its weather-beaten surface. Pre-Cambrian, geologists call them, and there is no older category in the study of the earth. Out of Pre-Cambrian hosts come some of the planet's richest ore-loads, and such has been the case in Australia where, it seems, there are still great discoveries waiting to be made.

Mineral finds, known ore reserves and output have increased dramatically over the past twenty years. In 1960 minerals ran to only about seven per cent of Australia's exports. By 1980 that figure had grown to some forty per cent and was rising. Oil and natural gas were the fields most explored and exploited. They had to be, for conditions in the Middle East were becoming more uncertain daily and Australia needed its fuel. By 1990 the country was producing eighty-five per cent of its oil needs: a far cry from the days when all oil was imported. Now Australia actually exports some twenty per cent of production.

Mines for other minerals, silver, copper, lead, tin, aluminium, uranium and zinc, litter the Australian continent. Silver was found in some areas with gold, and though it was not as valuable, diggers who were not striking it rich with anything else sank shafts into silver lodes. But Australia's silver city is undoubtedly Broken Hill. In 1883, the scent of recent gold rushes still in the air, Charles Rasp, riding a sheep station's boundary looking for lost sheep, eyed a hill with a broken top and thought there might be minerals there. He registered a claim and put down a shaft, hoping to find tin. What he discovered turned out to be an enormous load of silver and lead. It made Rasp rich, although he sold his share to a group of men who founded the Broken Hill Proprietary Company, which went on to become involved in steel and grew into Australia's largest company.

Broken Hill boomed. Eight years after Rasp laid his claim, the town had a population of almost twenty thousand, many of them immigrant miners who had not struck it rich elsewhere, men from Europe, Ireland, even from Malta, working in some of the worst underground conditions Australia has ever seen. Men died beneath the surface of the earth by the hundred. Those who survived the appalling danger of their work often died later of lead poisoning or lung disease brought on by the dry drilling that was practised, a method that filled the air they breathed with tons of poisonous dust. For years they fought to have wet drilling introduced — a constant flow of water into the drill-hole, washing away the dangerous ore, keeping down the dust. It took the miners thirty-five years to achieve success. It was not until the Big Strike of 1919 through 1920 that they finally got working conditions that were safer and a working week limited to thirty-five hours. And out of the miners' struggle grew another of the great Australian 'companies', the Barrier Industrial Council, the trade union which still very much runs the town today.

There are sharp black-and-white photographs of Broken Hill, taken at the time of the strike in 1919, showing hundreds of miners moving down, past heaps of ore, onto the delicate little colonial building that was the Broken Hill Proprietary office. Men formally dressed in suits, waistcoats, broad hats, some riding horses, some pushing bicycles, accompanied by their dogs, advance through the dust to make their protests, to claim more hope for their lives. In the end they succeeded. Today Broken Hill is a quiet town, a place of calm in the hard, hot land it sits on. Its street names are a catalogue of why it's there: Iodide Street, Chloride, Sulphide and Kaolin Streets cross Mica and Wolfram. Near the centre is Sturt Park, named after one of Australia's great explorers. Although in New South Wales, Broken Hill is so far west of Sydney its clocks register Adelaide, Central Time, not that of the east coast. The country as a whole is divided into three time zones, Eastern, Central and Western Standard Time. Eastern is ten hours ahead of Greenwich Mean Time, only half an hour ahead of Central and two hours ahead of Western.

Broken Hill is still the world's richest deposit of silver, lead and zinc. Some four hundred and fifty miles to the north-west lies the opal-producing centre of the world. Here, in South Australia's soft powdery landscape, the non-crystalline variety of silica the world knows as opal, with its delicate colours that glow when the stones are turned, is scratched out of the ground. Here, to escape the searing heat that parches the earth, many in the town of Coober Pedy live beneath the surface, seeking shelter the way the wombat does, in houses underground. Some of the dug-outs in the early days were exhausted mines, or mines that were still functioning but served a double purpose.

Coober Pedy, said by some to mean 'white man's hole' in an Aboriginal tongue, is one of Australia's most curious Outback towns. These days homes are deliberately cut from the earth not only to provide shelter but to add to the quietness of the place. Coober Pedy needs every touch of glamour it can get. Seen from a distance in shimmering heat, it looks like a mirage of desolation. Piles of rusting metal, car bodies, worn-

Driving to the Exhibition from Flinders-street Railway Station, Melbourne, 1888

out domestic appliances, litter the dusty earth. It is a scene from a catastrophe movie and was used as such in *Mad Max III*. Coober Pedy has another characteristic unusual for a mining community — there is no big mining company, there are no unions doing battle for their men.

Government policy allows a miner to stake a claim of no more than fifty square metres at a time; nor can large partnerships be built up. As a result, men work alone or in tiny groups, chipping away at the sandstone that holds the raw opal, formed in hollows or cracks in the sandstone, sometimes in pieces of fossil wood or shells or bones. By this policy the government is preventing any large-scale uprooting of the opal source. Only a fraction of it has been touched by the dust-covered men who dig in one hole during the working day, then crawl out of it and into another when it's time to take a rest. On Sundays they can attend a church carved out of subterranean rock. It's cool and peaceful, the acoustics are good, the saints hang serenely on the rocky walls.

Australia's mineral wealth seems endless. The country almost rings with iron. There are iron mountains where, they say, there's a danger of them going rusty when it rains. Australia is now the largest producer of iron ore in the world. Diamonds, first found in New South Wales in the 1860s, were mined for some years and then the workings were abandoned, because they were considered exhausted or unprofitable. However, in 1978, a major new discovery was made near Kimberley in Western Australia. The nation now produces over twelve per cent of the world's rough diamonds and there is talk of it becoming number one for industrial gems.

Whenever mining production figures are updated they seem to multiply enormously. The output of bauxite, the ore from which aluminium is extracted, has increased twelve fold in recent years, and manganese ore-yield by thirteen times, while coal production, which has always been high, has doubled — Australia now produces as much as Britain and Germany combined. Much of the new mineral wealth has been discovered in Western Australia, giving that state a new lease of economic life. Captain James Stirling's faith in that part of the country is at long last fully justified. Perth is now said to be every Australian's second favourite city, that's to say, the one they like best after their own. Unless, of course, you live there, then it's number one.

Out of the Sea

Australia's six varied seas have given the nation a huge range of wealth and sustenance, adventure, fun and vivid beauty. From the tropical north, down both bulging coasts, to the southern shoreline, fish and shellfish, seals, whales, all other creatures of the deep, have been taken since the first Aborigines walked the land. Whaling and sealing were among the colonies' early enterprises. Within ten years of the founding of New South Wales, seal skins had been collected by the thousand and whales were being slaughtered for their oil and for baleen, the springy mouth bone used by corset manufacturers to trim elegant ladies' waists. And, as in other parts of the world where they have been hunted, these often gentle, easily approached mammals of the sea were reduced in numbers almost to extinction.

When the white man settled along Australia's southern coast, in quiet coves and estuaries along Tasmania's shore, there were so many black whales that at times the settlers could almost walk across their backs. These were mostly female black whales who came north from Antarctica to calve in the calm coastal Australian and New Zealand waters. They were killed by the million, so that within forty years bay-whaling, as it came to be known, hardly existed as a trade. The same fate was dealt out to the seals, only they did not last as long. After they were clubbed to death, their skins were taken, sometimes their fat for oil, and the rest was left to rot. By 1826, George Arthur, Lieutenant-Governor of Van Diemen's Land, as Tasmania was called at the time, had become concerned that 'this valuable trade is threatened with speedy and total annihilation'.

That did not stop the slaughter. Nor did it make much impression on the men involved. There were American whalers who had come down from Boston, there were hard-boned clubbers and skinners who lived brutal lives, there were escaped convicts who joined the seal gangs, the sea rats, who had taken over part of Australia's coastline. Robert Hughes, in his well-written, excellently researched *The Fatal Shore*, refers to part of it as 'a veritable rookery of absconders', where men lived like pirates in 'patriarchal clans'. They stole Aborigine women to complete their tribes, for sex and for their skill as seal hunters. They ruled their small domains until the seals had been eliminated, until some more stable settlement found room for them. In the land's mythology, there are tales of how they cut off women's ears if they tried to escape the clan, and made them eat pieces of their own flesh to bind them to their 'owners'.

In today's world, a fisherman's life is hard but rarely quite as brutal, although appalling practices still exist. The way sharks, caught for their fins, are treated off Australia's or any other coast, is as monstrous as the clubbing of seal. The popularity in Asia of shark-fin soup, coupled with a lesser demand for the rest of the great fish, has given rise to what is known as 'finning'. The shark is caught, hauled aboard and the fins cut off. Then what's left of the beautiful, streamlined creature is dumped overboard. Without its fins, it sinks to die of starvation, shock or bleeding on the ocean floor. In what is supposed to be an enlightened age, this is a practice that should undoubtedly be banned.

Tuna, which are caught and kept whole, is big business in Australian waters, accounting for about thirty per cent of the country's total catch. Tons are swung ashore, hooked by their tails to cranes, on an almost daily basis. Most of it is canned and sent overseas. Another big Australian export from the sea is the line of frozen lobster tails that stretches almost all around the world. Crayfish, the locals call these large crustaceans, are not the classic lobster, they don't have the big bulbous claws, but they are big all over and have weighed in at twenty kilos or more. Unfortunately for them, they're delicious.

Out of the past and into the present has come another of the trades that links Australia to the sea. Pearling, which began off the nation's coast in the 1880s, continues today if not in quite the same manner. The old luggers, twin-masted, heavy-bellied sailing boats, and the divers that went down from their decks made Broome, high on the coast in Western Australia, the world's largest pearling centre in 1910. The oysters with the pearls they formed (usually to make a grain of sand they couldn't remove more comfortable to live with) and the shiny incurves of their shells, lay in beds some four miles off-shore. Of the two treasures the oyster produced, the shell-interior, the mother-of-pearl, was the bigger source of income. But it cost the early divers much to gain. Many died of the 'bends', the decompression sickness caused by bubbles in the bloodstream when the diver was pulled up too quickly. In 1914 alone, thirty-three divers fell victim. And the weather could be unfriendly. In 1908 one hundred and fifty pearlers died in a tropical cyclone.

Today's pearlers lead a less dangerous life. After years of depression when plastics replaced mother-of-pearl, Broome is once again a world pearling centre, thanks to the 'cultured' pearl industry, whereby the grain of sand is popped into the oyster, and time and the shellfish do the rest. There are some half a dozen pearl-culture farms in the warm waters near Broome, an irony really as the industry was developed by the Japanese who, in 1942, made an attempt to bomb Broome off the map. Now they have given it a flourishing business, Broome thrives as never before.

But perhaps the greatest pleasure to be gained from Australia's jewels in the sea is simply looking at them, diving down into the coral of the Great Barrier Reef, drifting through the multi-coloured, multi-layered forms of life to be found there. It is a thrill that can be enjoyed by all who tackle it, from the old to the very young. A group of islands off the north-east Queensland coast have been turned into tourist resorts. There, on a series of tiny specks of land that range from true islands — mountain tops projecting above the sea — to sand-filled cays or coral-heads, you can scuba-dive or snorkel, drift with goggles looking down, or be taken on a semi-sub, a craft with a deep hull and windows to look out of, as if you were a goldfish in a bowl put in the sea.

There you may see, in the hollows and caverns, the turns or the shadows of enormous coral heads, rainbow after rainbow of beautifully coloured fish, showers of blues and yellows, stripes of black and green. In the blue translucent distance, a grouper may move into the darkness of a cave, a turtle may paddle slowly up to the surface of the sea. This, the largest structure in the world built by living organisms, is enjoyed for what it is, a wonderland of nature, full of delicate life.

And away, on the far side of Australia, some two thousand miles or more west, another contact with nature lies waiting for those who wet their feet in Australian waters. In Shark Bay, north of Perth, is a beach called Monkey Mia where dolphins come up to swimmers, give them a nudge and say hello. They like to have their backs scratched and will take a fish or two almost as if to say they are prepared to forgive man for all the things he's done. 'But watch it, sport,' they also murmur. 'Keep your nose clean from now on.'

Brighton Beach, Melbourne, 1880

LIFE AND TIMES

The Sporting Scene

Australia is a sporting nation in every sense of the word. The wide outdoors, warm waters, acres of sunshine, and also generous government encouragement, have given rise to a host of champions, to varied and unusual sporting events, even the celebration of the 1956 Olympic Games on Australian soil. Australia proclaimed 1993 the Year of Sport, inviting all the world to come and watch everything in action, from the thoroughbreds in the Melbourne Cup to camels at Alice Springs.

From the early days of the colonies Australians have competed to win. A taste for sport came to the country with the First Fleet in 1788; the challenge thrown down in order to survive gave it a cutting edge. Boxing matches, sometimes between Currency lads and Sterling intruders, were brutal, bloody affairs. Bare-knuckled pugilists smashed at each other for twenty-five rounds or more, shouted on by eager spectators, 'jolly dogs' as they were called in a billboard of the day.

Not only men were matched against each other. Cockfights, although illegal, were held from time to time, even if it meant risking arrests and fines, so eager were the early settlers for something to entertain them. Dogs were pitted against dogs, sometimes dogs against possums — a match in 1829 ended in a draw. But somewhat more civilised events were also being organised. In 1810 the first horse races were held in Sydney and the beginnings of a long tradition were laid down.

There are race courses in every city in Australia, in every country town, but the most famous is in Melbourne where, on the first Tuesday of each November, the famous Cup is raced for. The event is such a part of the nation's fabric that the day is an official holiday in the state of Victoria and an unofficial one just about everywhere else. *Sickies* are thrown all over the country to get the day off. Australians have a nice touch when it comes to producing a word or phrase that fits. A tea-break is often a *smoko*. When you're off on your sickie, you're *crook*; when getting better, you're 'coming good'. My favourite is *garbo*, the name given to the man who collects the garbage.

Australian sporting heroes, and there are many, are not only the nation's men and women. One of the greatest was Phar Lap, a famous chestnut racehorse which was, in fact, New Zealand bred. The winner of thirty-seven races, including the 1930 Melbourne Cup, the animal took the nation's heart and, in the end, they had his. Phar Lap died after winning a race in New Mexico, and Australia, mourning his loss, pointed an accusing finger at the United States. After the valiant gelding's mysterious death, he was brought back and divided. Today his stuffed hide is on display in Melbourne, his heart in Canberra, and his skeleton in Wellington, New Zealand. No other sporting hero has been quite so completely shared. And there have been many.

One of the earliest was Don Bradman, cricketer supreme. Bradman, later Sir Donald, the only Australian so far knighted for hitting a ball with a bat, set a formidable number of records in the game, including the highest score — his personal best was 452 when playing for New South Wales against Queensland in the 1929-30 season. He led his country to victory several times to win what is known as the Ashes. A curious trophy in the shape of an urn, the Ashes came into being after an Australian team beat England on English soil in 1882. The *Sporting Times* published an epitaph lamenting the death of English Cricket, saying that the body would be cremated and the ashes taken to Australia. When an English team paid a return visit to Australia and won, it was presented with an urn containing ashes. So the sequence began. The Ashes, like the remains of Phar Lap, seem a little like morbid trophies of times past, although Australian sport today is

208. Sydney's centre is a jumble of building styles, a mixed growth that began in the melting pot of colonial development. Australia's first official architect was Francis Greenway. Greenway was a convict sentenced for forgery, but there was nothing counterfeit about his work in Sydney. He designed many handsome Georgian buildings and recommended that future streets be laid down on a grid pattern, the basic plan that exists in the city today.

209, 210. Sydney's magnificent harbour was not Captain Phillip's first choice when he landed in 1788. He went first to Botany Bay, ten miles to the south, but failed to find the rolling grasslands, the well-watered trees, he had been told awaited him there. Instead there was dry scrubland, spindly eucalyptus, Aborigines who shouted and flung spears. Phillip waited for the rest of the First Fleet to join him then moved north to Port Jackson, where he was satisfied with what he saw and founded the town of Sydney. Even so, hard times lay ahead. The early settlers almost starved. It was not until the end of the century that Sydney began to flourish. (pp. 250-253)

Playing for Keeps

alive and well.

Eight million Aussies, more or less half the population, are registered as taking part in the sporting life. The list of things they do and dabble in is as long as a bowler's arm — be that cricket, baseball or lawn-bowling. Every sport of the sea, the surf, the sand, is followed by increasing numbers of tanned Australians with sun-bleached hair. Conscious of the diminishing ozone layer — the country has one of the highest skin cancer rates in the world — they paint their noses with zinc paste, to keep the sun away.

The nation's 1983 victory in the America's Cup yacht race is perhaps the highlight of their playing with wind and wave. The fact that it was won back by the Americans four years later took away none of Down Under's glory. The country's victory over the Yanks was the first in the Cup's history. To win it back, the American team had to sail off the coast of Western Australia, making Fremantle, briefly, the centre of the sailing world.

Away from the sea, up in the snow, Australia has more working snow fields than there are in Switzerland. The snows of the Snowy Mountains, where Australia's ski-runs lie, give rise to the headwaters of a number of rivers on which the great Snowy River Scheme was based in 1949. While not exactly a sporting event, the project became the subject of a determinedly-played political game. Devised by the Labor Government, it was designed to divert water westward, under the Australian Alps, to irrigate fruit-growing and grazing districts in Victoria and New South Wales. As it flowed west, instead of east, the water dropped some six hundred feet, generating electricity. Because it was a Labor scheme, the conservative Liberal-Country Party coalition wanted nothing to do with it at all — until they were in power. Then Menzies, adroit politician that he was, claimed it as the greatest single piece of public works in the nation's history. Today it supplies about twenty per cent of Australia's electrical power and irrigates thousands of acres of agricultural soil.

Australians have always enjoyed the kicking game, political or otherwise, which is perhaps why football in various forms draws the biggest crowds. Rugby, soccer and Rugby League all have their followings, but none so devoted as those in Victoria, and other southern states, who cheer on the eighteen-man-a-side teams playing Australian Rules. Developed in 1858 by T.W. Willis, a well-known cricketer, and his cousin H.G. Harrison as a game to play in the winter months, it was loosely based on the rules of Rugby, using a similar ball. However as the colonies' football fields were made of harder stuff than those in rainy England, it became a much more open game. There's a lot of jumping and kicking involved. There are no scrums, line-outs or off-side rules, and the players usually perform in sleeveless shirts. Crowds of more than one hundred thousand turn out to watch important matches.

Whether it's hang-gliding, bungee-jumping, wood-chopping or racing craft made from empty beer cans, Aussies are always ready to have a go. Often they compete in easy companionship, at times in a grimmer mood, especially when the nation's reputation is at stake. But they've always had a good name as sportsmen and women, and there is probably no other country of similar population size that has known quite the same success.

Australia is a gambling nation, some say the heaviest in the world. Hardly surprising, since readiness to take risks must have been a quality shared by many of those early settlers who set sail from England into the

211. The transformation of Darling Harbour from run-down docklands to Sydney's leisure centre took four years and two billion dollars to complete. The old rat-infested wool-sheds and crumbling wharves were turned into a series of restaurants, shops and bars, the site for the Sydney Aquarium, Chinese Garden and National Maritime Museum — all a world away from the dilapidated vestiges of another age, a rebirth the city is justifiably proud of.

212, 213. Darling Harbour was named after Ralph Darling, governor of New South Wales from 1825 to 1831. In spite of the fact that Darling was unpopular, and all Sydney celebrated when he was abruptly recalled, he not only had a harbour named after him but a river, a range of mountains and a series of rolling downs as well.

214. *Sydney's skyline is ever-changing; cranes are constantly at work. It is difficult to imagine that slightly over 200 years ago this was an empty shore. Even the Aborigines built nothing permanent – a few bark shelters that blew down, little more. When the first white men began construction, they cut down trees, built rough houses with sun-baked bricks. Now Sydney covers more than 1500 square miles and is home to more than 3.5 million people.*

215. One symbol of Sydney's growth is the
Opera House. In the 1950s, the prize for its
design was won by a Dane. For years
Danish, English and Australian structural
engineers worked on how the swooping
roof-line might be built. When construction
began, tiles came from Sweden, panes of
glass from France. Stage lighting was
imported from Germany, electronic equipment from the USA. Finally opened by the
Queen, the building now is Sydney's pride.

216, 217. Sydney, a still-rising city, was virtually the capital of the country until Australia became a Commonwealth. Even after Canberra was established as the seat of federal government, Sydney continued to grow, to develop a patchwork of suburbs stitched together like a many-coloured quilt. Today it is more cosmopolitan than any other Australian city and, at the same time, has become truly integrated-Australian. The suburb of Redfern, for example, not so long ago an inner-city slum, has been taken over by Aborigines, who have renovated houses, painted ethnic murals, and brought a fresh vitality to the area. They, and others like them, make Sydney one of the most exciting cities in the Western world.

218. Australians are a prosperous people. They may dress casually but they dress well, as these pedestrians crossing a busy Sydney street display. Good wages are maintained by powerful trade unions, to which the majority of workers belong.

219. In the heart of Sydney the monorail hurries through the city centre. Most Australians, however, own cars: 80 per cent of households have one car, 30 per cent own two, and a high seven per cent, three. Overall, that is a rate second only to the United States.

220, 221. Not part of the Statue of Liberty nor a computer game but aspects of Auditorium Square in Adelaide, South Australia. Adelaide, which had a reputation of being the most restrained and conservative of all the nation's capitals, seemed to break old bonds when the Festival Centre, which includes Auditorium Square, was designed.

222. South, over the Opera House (overleaf), lie some of Sydney's most prized residential suburbs in a glorious setting.

263

223, 224. Melbourne, capital of Victoria, was founded in 1835 by Batman — John Batman, a Tasmanian settler who acquired land on the banks of the Yarra River because it was a good place, he thought, to start a 'village'. Batman purchased the land from a group of Aborigines, a deal that was later declared illegal, one of the reasons being that, as the natives had no legal right to any part of the land that England had claimed, they were not in a position to sell it. Melbourne, however, survived. As its soaring skyline shows, it has come some way from Batman's village.

225. Melbourne's skyline has risen dramatically in the past few years as its population has risen to over 3 million. Here, high-lifting reflections shimmer in the Yarra River, around which the city spreads. Tucked away are nineteenth-century buildings, conservative and elegant, like the soul of the city itself. Melbourne has been called English, intellectual, and sporting mad. All labels apply, but there is a solidness about Melbourne that is not quite as apparent elsewhere in Australia.

226. *The nineteenth century encircled by the late twentieth — a combination Australia has come to know. Here, in Melbourne's centre, glass provides the backdrop to Victorian brick; repeated columns enclose intricate design. Fewer of Melbourne's older buildings have been replaced than is the case in Sydney. Enough remain in the heart of the city, the Golden Mile, to keep the flavour of times past alive and well.*

227. *The Shrine of Remembrance, Melbourne's principal monument to those who died in foreign wars, stands in King's Domain, one of the city's many parks and gardens. Kings Domain, in a great sweep south of the Yarra River, encloses Government House, the Botanical Gardens, the Old Observatory and the National Herbarium. It is a green and gentle parkland, set beside the water, full of life and memory, the ebbing of time.*

228. *On the corner of Melbourne's Spring and Little Bourke Streets is the Princess Theatre, resplendent with its royal coat of arms. Built in 1877 to commemorate Queen Victoria's half century on the throne, its elaborate touches of Victoriana have remained unaltered down the years. The productions, however, have changed with time. Instead of 'Lady Windermere's Fan' one is much more likely to see 'Cats' or 'The Rocky Horror Show'.*

229, 230. The stamp of England, impressed so deeply during the first 150 years of growth, remains clearly recognisable in many Australian suburban streets. Away from city centres, façades speak of small shopkeepers, services, places of recreation. This is Melbourne, but it could be an English town or somewhere in Canada, New Zealand, even the United States. Until the end of WW II most migrants came from the 'Old Country' or the 'Old Dart' as it was sometimes called, and their roots were strong. Almost everyone had an aunt in England, a grandfather in Ireland, relatives in Scotland. The trip 'home' was a standard pilgrimage.

231, 233. Canberra is one of the few cities in the world built to a plan. Ten years after the colonies federated in 1901, its site, 200 miles south-west of Sydney, was selected as the seat of a national government. A world-wide competition was held for a city design, won, in 1913, by Walter Burley Griffin, an American. Building began slowly. It was not until 1927 that the first Federal Parliament assembled in the capital, and that was only in a 'temporary location'. In 1988 this 'permanent' New Parliament House was opened, it too the result of an international competition, this time won by an Italian.

232. Canberra's Old Parliament House, the 'temporary' site where Australia's Federal Parliament sat for 61 years. Because of the fierce rivalry between Sydney and Melbourne, when the country became a Commonwealth Canberra was selected as somewhere diplomatically distant from both.

234. *Miles of golden Queensland sand, blue skies, towering accommodation blocks — Surfers Paradise. In 1936 there was just one hotel isolated by the shore. Today, in the afternoon sun, much of the beach is shadowed by the high-risers jammed along the coastline.*

235. *Melbourne has also seen remarkable change in the past half century — and much of that has been upward. Although a city of parks and gardens, where one acre in four is left as greenspace, Melbourne's skyline has leapt to the clouds as this network of steel exemplifies.*

236. A bustling street filled with customers, traffic, shops and services. It happens to be Fremantle, but it could be almost anywhere in the country. The majority of Australians, 85 per cent of the total population, live in urban areas; about 70 per cent own or are buying their homes. Australians are cared for from cradle to grace. Medicare helps those who need it. Between 1909 and 1912, old age and invalid pensions and maternity allowances were introduced — a move that was considered pioneering at the time.

ESTAB · 1882

THE CAIRNS POST PTY. LTD.

237. The Cairns Post, one of the older newspapers, is part of an active network. Australia has one of the highest readerships of periodicals in the world. Colour TV is available to 99 per cent of the population. TV stations use a high proportion of Australian-produced material. Radio goes into almost every home. Australian films, boosted by government aid, have scored high marks internationally. Radio Australia, the overseas short-wave service, broadcasts in nine languages to Asia and the Pacific.

THEIR NAME LIVETH
FOR EVERMORE

238. The Australian War Memorial, Canberra, is one of the country's many monuments to those who died in war. Yet it is more. It is a study of war itself. Maps of battles, the weapons used, even the role of the media are explained and presented. Both World Wars are featured, as are Korea and Vietnam.

239. Canberra, set in the Australian Capital Territory (ACT), is also a pleasure-ground of parks and gardens, of free-standing sculpture, old and new — this one is the Navy Memorial. The capital's population has risen from 50,000 in 1960 to nearly 300,000.

240. Rising like some creature from the deep, multi-helmeted, many-jawed, the Sydney Opera House seems to gnaw at the Harbour Bridge. There has never been a building in Australia's short, vivid history that has aroused so much controversy. Danish-designed, built in the first civilised Aborigine's backyard, plagued with technical problems, financed by the country's gambling fever, the construction took twenty years to complete. Yet today the white shell-roofed structure is the most famous opera house in the world. Performers travel the lengths of the earth to play and sing in its lofty halls. In short, it is a success.

unknown. In many ways it's been gambling ever since. Perhaps the most ambitious bet was the opening of the nation's doors to millions of immigrants after World War II. This is a wager the country has won, even though it has profoundly changed its character. Now Melbourne has the third largest Greek community on the planet. King's Cross, just over the hill from the heart of Sydney, has Japanese, Italian, Mexican, French, Indonesian and Hare Krishna-vegetarian restaurants, among others, standing cheek by munching jowl. Down Queensland's Gold Coast, a twenty-mile strip of commercialised paradise with two million visitors a year, forty per cent of the hotel rooms are owned by the Japanese. And even Perth, on Australia's west coast, once James Stirling's dream of Little England, Hesperia he wanted to call it, will never be the same after the American invasion leading up to their regaining of the America's Cup in 1987.

While tastes in food and drink may have changed, one aspect of the Aussie character has remained intact: the willingness to wager, to bet on anything that moves, even two flies crawling up a wall. It was this desire to have a punt that paid for the Sydney Opera House. Through the lottery organised to finance the project, more than two hundred million Australian dollars were raised. Every state has its lottery, and betting on horses is almost endemic. Even bookmakers are respected; they're often referred to as turf accountants.

But the most Aussie of all is two-up, a basic pitch and toss. Two pennies, old fashioned, none of the decimal coinage, with Queen Victoria on the head if possible, are tossed into the air from a wooden stick, a kip it's called in the game. If the pennies land with two heads up, the spinner has won. Two tails is a loss. A head and a tail means another spin. The game is as simple and as fascinating as that. It's also illegal, which adds to its charm. I was taken to a game in Sydney once, to an old two-storied house in an inner suburb, one of the dwellings in a row with cast-iron balconies, heavy metal that had been brought out to the colonies a hundred years before as ballast in the holds of ships.

The front door was opened by a thick-set man who, after eyeing me, let us into what was no longer a two-storey house but a gambling barn with sand on the floor; the partitioning walls and floors had been taken away, leaving only the outer walls. They were lined by men, some squatting, some standing, with more money than I have ever seen in my life, before or since. The wooden kip, polished by hundreds of gamblers' hands, went from spinner to spinner in turn. Each had three chances to toss up heads; each time the money was doubled. Those around the ring bet against the spinner and bet amongst themselves. There were no women present. There was very little said. It was a game as intense as a religious meeting, taken as solemnly as an oath. Whenever anyone won a large enough bet, ten per cent went to the house. I can't recall if I won or lost, but I will never forget the earnestness of the occasion.

The Social Game

Whether taking their sport seriously or gambling in fun, Australians have adequate time to enjoy their pursuits. Every employed person is entitled to four or five weeks' paid holiday a year. Public holidays are usually taken on a Monday or Friday, giving a long weekend. There is plenty to do on the Australian landscape, urban, suburban or out in the sticks, and the people are doing more of it together, sharing their free time.

Not very long ago leisure activities were things that jokers did.

Sheilas didn't belong. That is to say, it was a masculine world, women stayed at home. It was a long time before women were allowed into the boozer to drink side by side with men. They had their own little nooks away in a corner, called Ladies' Parlours or something equally polite, but they were not part of the big, white-tiled bars where men stood, at times with a glass in each hand and a bottle under their arm. Until the licensing hours were altered, pubs closed about six in the evening, which gave the working man only an hour's drinking time. It was enough, to fill his boots, to shout — that is, to pay for his round, and to stagger out the door when 'Closing Time' was called. The streets outside many city pubs at that time in the evening were not a pretty sight. Children avoided them. 'Respectable' citizens, their noses in the air, walked the other side of the road. The only women present were those who were there to collect their men, to bundle them home.

Such Hogarthian scenes are gone now, although a curious relic remains. A large number of Australian restaurants are not licensed to serve drink with the food they provide. They are known as BYO restaurants and advertise as such. You take whatever you want to drink and the restaurant will open it for you, though they may charge a corkage fee. BYO stands for Bring Your Own. Sometimes a G is added, in case you haven't realised that what they meant was Grog.

Separate areas for the sexes was not confined to bars. Odd as it may seem, there was a time when dance halls had rows of seats down either side, one for the women, the other for the men. (In some of the country dance-palaces, there was a different division: one side was for the townies and the other for those who belonged to the cattle stations, were part of the squatter class.) However, most men just hung around in groups waiting for the music to start. Then they flung down the cigarettes they were smoking, stamped out the buts and made for the girl they fancied as fast as they could, hurrying to beat anyone else with the same idea. They danced, returned their partner to her seat and often, with admirable foresight, reserved the last dance, hoping for an opportunity to escort the lady home.

But that, too, is a snapshot of the past, however close or far. Australia,

Sheep-shearing in the late nineteenth century

282

like the rest of the western world, began to alter fundamentally in the 1970s. Immigrants, with their diverse lifestyles, helped to bring about the change. The sexual revolution, long hair, drugs, and rock-and-roll, all played their part. The media, especially television, knitted all those who spoke English, or any other language, a little more tightly, bound the simple stitches of purl and plain into a more complicated design.

Women, having demanded their rights, and been granted them, began to invade the male strongholds. Bars these days are no longer the cavernous, white-walled urinals they used to resemble not so long ago. Most are comfortable places to have a drink, to sit at a table on a carpeted floor, a woman by your side, or well-shaded beer gardens with somewhere for the children to play. There is still the occasional bloodhouse, as the old-style boozer was sometimes called, and there are also those with Ladies' Lounges, but they are fossils rather than the living breed.

Dancing is as New Age as it is anywhere else on earth. Discotheques are as sophisticated or as unruly as any in the world; there is no longer the stampede toward the sheilas when the first notes hit the air. Even the last bastions of Australian male totemism, the surf clubs and horse-racing's inner circle, have been opened, albeit reluctantly, to the fair ladies of the land.

Jockey clubs have their counterparts in other countries, but the Aussie surf-lifesaver is very much the nation's own. He goes back almost to the beginning of the century. At Bondi, one of Sydney's beaches, the Surf-Bather's Lifesaving Club was founded in 1906. Sydney's beaches, like others around Australia's coast, take the full force of the open sea. Waves pound in, crash onto the sand, drag themselves away to begin again. Undercurrents can be deadly. Nineteenth-century swimmers seldom ventured from the shallows, but then they also wore long-sleeved garments and wide-brimmed hats to protect themselves from the sun. When they finally took to the water and some were drowned, out of the shadows of the Australian bush, from the pool of black beneath the ghost gum tree, stepped the man from which myths were made in the shape of a bronzed life-saver.

There was something military about them. They were the thin tanned line between the danger in the churning waves and the safety of the shore. As they patrolled the beaches, they wore uniforms in the form of bathing suits and coloured scull-caps tied beneath the chin. Their courage was, and still is, beyond all question; they saved many a swimmer's life. And perhaps the parades they mounted, the drills they practised on the sand, the way they marched in military style, had much to do with the co-ordination needed at times of danger, with the teamwork rapid action required. But they also became known as a very *macho* mob. No women were wanted in their ranks.

Maybe this attitude was, in part, forced upon them. Questions had been raised about the very act of lying openly in the sun. Archbishop Kelly, one of Australia's leading Catholic voices of 1911, publicly worried about 'promiscuous commingling of the sexes' the new pastime encouraged. So perhaps the surfers closed ranks against the fair sex by unpopular demand, and only touched them publicly when they were dragged, half-drowned, ashore. However, that too, has gone. Women now brave the seas, take part in surfboat races, hauling the five-oared open row-boat out through the waves, round marker buoys and back to shore. They participate in staged rescue exercises, running the cord attached to the life-saver through one hand held on top of their heads, pulling saver and victim back out of the surf, breathing life back into the 'drowning' swimmer. Later they will share a tube or two of lifesaving liquid, Australia's splendid beer. The sheilas

have moved into the joker's world and they reckon they're there to stay.

But Australian women's rise toward the equality they have achieved has not been easy. Even though a Sex Discrimination Act was written into law in 1984, it took a determined, at times bitter, strike by nurses in Victoria to get the working conditions *they* believed were really equal, to be treated the same as men. It is not surprising that one of the strongest and most intelligent voices in the women's movement internationally is that of Germaine Greer, who understands clearly the power of the written word.

The written word in Australia goes back to colonial times. Broadsheets, journals, pamphlets, were printed from almost the first days of settlement in New South Wales. The press, and what is now called the media, grew at a healthy rate. Australia is a literate nation, with one of the highest readerships of newspapers and periodicals of any country in the world. One of the first to make its mark, to set a standard that was neither high nor low but always acceptable, was the *Australian Women's Weekly*. The first issue, in 1933, called for 'Equal Social Rights for SEXES'. The journal went on to become an institution. It and others like it, such as the weekly *Bulletin* for men, were read the length and breadth of the land.

Those were the days before television came to claim the time, days when the local lending library was always full. It was a centre of gossip, a way to pass a moment or two of pleasant time, the place to pick up the latest book, or to put your name on the waiting list if it wasn't available.

Then in 1956, to coincide with the Olympic Games, TV arrived on Australia's turf and, once again, the country altered. Like everywhere else in the literate world, book readers had their attention drawn elsewhere, cinema audiences had less need to leave their living rooms, the show came into the home. Now there are two hundred and fifty TV stations in Australia, five on the ground in Sydney alone, and that's not counting satellite programmes that beam in from outer space. Some Australian stations are ethnic, 'multi-cultural' is the politically correct term, to cover the New Australians, particularly those from the Asian north, who have changed the country's character more than the media could ever hope to.

A dinkum Aussie in the 1990s might be a Vietnamese greengrocer with stacks of shining fruit, a Lebanese mechanic with blackened fingernails, a Spanish carpet salesman trying to make his small business grow, an English art gallery director excited about the work he sees, or an Aborigine rock star jumping in paint and jeans. All are part of the nation, all speak, if they've been in the country long enough, with the dragged-out vowels of the Australian drawl. They are the nation now — a far cry from the first settlers who waded ashore, some armed, some chained, all bewildered by the land before them, the line of blackfellows along the shore.

The First-fleeters ran up the British flag, claimed the colony for the Crown, drank toasts to George III, King of England, Defender of the Faith. Today's Australian is no longer required to pledge loyalty to the Queen: to the country and its Constitution is enough. She or he no longer sings *God Save the Queen* at official functions; *Advance Australia Fair*, the current national anthem, represents the nation as a whole.

And one day soon all Australians, old and new, might well belong to a republic with no official ties to England, with no attachment to any Crown. Bloodlines, heartlines, will link them to the country that many once thought of as 'Home', the 'Old Dart', the land that belonged to their forefathers but will have little to do with their sons. Paul Keating, who became Prime Minister at the end of 1991, favours the concept of Republic Australia, a step that would require the support of the majority of the people, to be voted on when the moment comes. That moment may not be distant. By the year 2000, Keating believes, the time of separation will have come.

In its relatively brief life as part of the greater world, Australia has seen many changes, some rapid, some violent, some harmoniously brought about. All have introduced new life and attitudes, new skills and creative ideas. Not all have been welcomed, but most have come to stay. It remains to be seen what alterations lie ahead, what new impetus might change the course of the slowly-drifting island-continent. Australia has been called the lucky country. Long may the label stick!

CHRONOLOGY

c. 40,000	First Aborigines come down from S.E. Asia
c. 1520	Portuguese may have landed in Victoria
1606	Dutchman, Janssen, explores Cape York
1623	Dutch return, name Arnhem and Carpentaria
c. 1628	Dutch now call the country New Holland
1642	Abel Tasman names Tasmania Van Diemen's Land, but sees no future in the country
1688-89	Englishman, Dampier, makes two voyages but, like the Dutch, considers country worthless
1770	Englishman Cook lands at Botany Bay, claims east coast for England, names it New South Wales
1788	Phillip establishes English penal colony
1794	Macarthur begins cross-breeding sheep, establishes the country's wool industry
1801	Flinders begins circumnavigation of the continent, recommends it be called Australia
1808	Rum Rebellion, Bligh imprisoned
1810	Macquarie begins to reform and develop colony
1817	Bank of New South Wales established, currency issued
1824	Brisbane penal colony for 'worst class of convicts'
1829	Stirling founds Perth, Western Australia, as free settlement
1835	Melbourne established as another free settlement
1840	Transport of felons 'officially' ends
1843	Australia's first free elections, men only
1844	More felons land 'quietly'; Leichhardt explores the north
1849	Hostile crowds protest the arrival of more convicts
1851	Anti-Transportation League founded; gold rushes begin
1854	Battle of Eureka Stockade
1859	Queensland separates, giving Australia six colonies
1860-61	Burke and Wills cross from Melbourne to north coast, die on return journey
1868	End of transportation
1880	Capture and death of Ned Kelly
1901-02	Australia becomes a Commonwealth, White Australia Policy passes into law, women get right to vote
1904	First Labour government
1913	Canberra named Federal capital
1914	Australia declares war on Germany
1915	Anzacs land at Gallipolli, nearly 8000 Australians die
1916	Australia votes NO to military conscription
1918	Armistice ends World War I
1919	New Guinea, former German colony, mandated to Australia
1922	Settlement Act increases immigration
1927	Federal parliament established in Canberra
1928	Flying Doctor service begins for Outback patients
1929	Stock Market crash depression begins
1939	Australia declares war on Germany
1942	Japan enters World War II, takes Singapore, bombs Darwin, submarines attack Sydney

1949	Menzies begins 17-year term as Prime Minister, longest in country's history
1951	ANZUS pact signed between U.S.A., New Zealand and Australia
1956	Olympic Games in Melbourne
1962	Aborigines given right to vote
1965	Australian troops go to Vietnam
1966	Decimal currency introduced
1967	Prime Minister Harold Holt disappears while swimming
1972	Labour back in power
1973	Sydney Opera House opened by Queen Elizabeth II
1975	Gough Whitlam, Labour Prime Minister, removed from power by Governor General
1978	Northern Territory granted self-government
1984	'Advance Australia Fair' replaces 'God Save the Queen' as national anthem
1991	Paul Keating replaces Bob Hawke as Labour Prime Minister
1992	Oath of allegiance no longer includes reference to Queen

Captain James Cook, the celebrated navigator who claimed Australia for the British Crown in 1770

Index